COMPRESSIONS

"THE SECRETS OUT"

BEWARE OF YOUR ACTIONS THEY MAY HINDER YOUR FUTURE.

Javon Butler

"BEWARE OF THE HAND
YOU FALL IN LOVE WITH.
THAT HAND MAYBE
COVERED BY A GLOVE
BLINDING ITS TRUE TOUCH."

—JAVON BUTLER

4

CHAPTER 1.

As the spring breeze came rushing in from an open window, the slightly opened blinds left some space for the morning sunlight to seep through the room. It is just pass dawn and the birds have stopped singing when the sound of an alarm clock goes off. Austin relentlessly wakes up as he reached for the alarm clock. He makes his way back into his bed to see his beautiful wife of many years. "Good morning baby," he said to his wife Victoria. She opened her eyes looking at Austin and smiled. Victoria then sat up in the bed, stretching her arms while yawning. "Good morning babe. You were an animal last night." she replied. She then leaned over to kiss Austin on his chest. "You were amazing," she said looking at Austin as she laid on his chest. "I don't know if it was me or the wine, but you were very excited and I loved it," she told Austin with a twinkle in her eyes. "You know you always get me going baby. Besides, I had to put it down. Especially since we're having all this company today. It wouldn't be like I could just creep up on you while you're doing the dishes and get it going right there on the kitchen floor." "Babe you're nasty but I love it." she joked, while rolling off of Austin to sit up on the edge of the bed and looking back at him. "I'm not nasty baby." he replied. "I just know what I'm doing and I know what you like." Not convinced she believed him, he continued, "I'm serious. I know what you like. And to have to think about it and waiting all day would have drove me crazy." Cutting him off, she told Austin to shut up, as they both laughed. Then he asked, "Why are we having a cookout or whatever you want to call it, anyway?" Turning from looking at Austin, Victoria slowly stood up from the bed. She began putting on her silk red robe that she purposely wore for Austin last night. "Well, if you must know?" she said while raising her eyebrows and shrugging her shoulders. Austin then said, "What? What is it babe?" She ignored Austin and continued to tie her robe together. Then he blurted out, "Stop playing and just spit it out." "Ok, ok. Patrick is going to ask for your blessing to marry Jasmine." "What? Marry Jasmine? Why couldn't he just come over and have a beer and ask me? I've been knowing that boy for about two years now, if not more Victoria. I don't want all this emotional shit going on. I mean, I like the guy but why do you want to throw a party or whatever for that? I hope he don't ask me in front everyone... And how is that going to work? Is he going to ask me then ask Jasmine at the same time?" "No baby he's not. Stop being all bent out of shape. You should be happy for them." Victoria said as she walked towards the bedroom door. "I am. I just don't like all this extra stuff." Austin explained. "What do you mean?" She asked, turning and facing Austin. "I mean you know me baby. If I like you, I like you. If I don't, I don't. Plain and simple. We doing all this for nothing. What if I tell the kid no, then what? Everybody will look at me like I'm the bad guy because of my decision." Victoria then looked at Austin squinting her eyes and said, "If that's your decision you shouldn't worry about what people say." and walked out of the bedroom. Before she got down the hallway, Victoria turned back and walked to the bedroom door. "Oh, and for your information, this whole get together was my idea, not his. I put it all together so you wouldn't feel like it was too emotional. I figured he could ask you

6

over some beers and food so y'all can relax without it being in an intense environment. So when you said, 'I know you.' You were right. Austin Roberts you're always making a small thing into a big deal. You say it's plain and simple. It's more like, plain and simple to others because your ass is not plain nor simple." Victoria fussed as she walked away. "I'm getting in the shower," she yelled while laughing and saying "plain and simple, yeah right." By the time Victoria was down the hall, Austin had sat up on his side of the bed. Taking a deep breath, and talking to himself he said, "What a way to start a morning." Austin knew it was early and he didn't feel like getting chewed out by Victoria anymore. When she got out of the shower, he figured he would give her some time to get her attitude together. He reached over, grabbing his phone, and calling his long-time best friend, Thomas. They had known each other since middle school. Thomas and Austin were so close that they even graduated from the same college. Trying to get away from Vicky, he was wishing his friend would pick up the phone. Without a doubt, Thomas picked up. "Hello? You up?" Austin asked. "Damn man, I wasn't. It's early as hell. What's up?" "Man, I need a favor." Thomas replied sarcastically, "Sure what else is new." "I need to go to Lowe's and run some errands for this cookout today. Can you ride with me?" Austin asked. "Damn man, I knew I shouldn't have picked up." Thomas said with frustration in his voice. "What you mean you shouldn't have picked up?" Austin asked. "Your ass called back fast when I text you 'Victoria was trying to bribe me into having a cookout.' You always want to come eat up people shit but don't want to help do shit." Austin said as they both laughed. "Now come on, get up. I'm leaving to head to your house after I brush my teeth and wash my face." "Alright, alright... Damn, I'm getting up now man. I was having a dream about two butt naked hoes. Now I have to help your ass." Thomas complained. With a serious tone Thomas asked, "Hey A," (that's the nickname he called Austin from time to time.) Austin answered, "Yeah what's up?" "A, do you think it's something I can google to help me go back to the same dream? Them hoes was fine as hell." Thomas bust out laughing on the phone. Austin joined him saying, "Honestly, I hope it is. I was rich, single and about twenty years younger. I had two amazing chicks beside me on somebody's beach when I woke up to Vicky snoring beside me. Don't get me wrong, I love my baby, but I would dream that dream all over again every night if I could." They both started laughing again. Then Thomas said, "Yeah, you think you slick. I don't know if she was snoring this morning but I do know you're conniving and trying to get out the house." Man, what are you talking about?" Austin asked. "I know either two things happened; Victoria bust your bubble and made you look stupid, or she just getting on your nerves. Right now she's probably in the shower or at the mailbox. Damn, what I'm talking about. It's too early in the morning to be at a mailbox. Austin, she done bust your bubble early this morning and you trying to creep out while she's in the shower." Austin cut him off and said, "Man, shut up." They got quiet for a few seconds and Austin confessed, "She's in the shower. Are you going to help me or not?" Thomas then bust out laughing again and said, "Austin, you are a grown ass kid man. Show Vicky's ass who's the man. Who puts on the pants and who wears the panties?" "Man, shut up. I'll be there in like 30 minutes." Austin replied. "Alright." Thomas said still laughing as Austin hung up the phone. He jumped up and went into the other bathroom. He began rushing to brush his teeth and wash his face. He listened to see if the water stopped running in the other bathroom, hoping to be done before Victoria got out of the shower. He spit out the toothpaste, quickly washed his face and ran back to the bedroom. He went into his neatly organized walk in closet grabbing his favorite gray sweat suit and the first pair of sneakers he saw. Quickly, he began throwing it all on. As soon as he walked out of the closet, Austin heard the shower turn off. Nervously thinking, "Damn, I have to hurry up and leave." As soon as he made his way to the bedroom door, Victoria came walking out of the master bathroom. "And where do you think your black ass is going?" Victoria asked jokingly. Austin replied, "Well, you know baby, I have to go pick up some stuff for the grill. I know you wanted me to pick up some extra cups and things for the cookout." "Aww baby, look at you being all nice. I think that's a great idea but I was hoping you could help me out with something before our guests arrive." Victoria said. "Oh ok babe, no problem. What is it?" Austin asked. "Well you seem like you're on a mission." Victoria said looking Austin up and down as she raised her right eyebrow. "You're also already fully dressed. Guess I'll have to just wait until you get back." When she mentioned he was "already fully dressed," Austin knew she wanted that good ole morning loving. Austin was in shock that she was not mad. She even seemed like she had got over the small back and forth spat they just had. Austin started thinking, "why the hell was I really trying to leave in the first place?" The conversation was not really a big deal. He then realized, "Vicky was right. I do blow things up for no reason." Standing there, staring at Victoria as she stood in front him. Still dripping from the shower and looking incredible. A sense of regret came over him. Austin hated that he was going to have to wait for the morning loving that will now turn into an afternoon quickie because of the cookout. He thought to himself, "I should have never put these damn clothes on." Austin thought Victoria was the most beautiful woman on earth and it drove him crazy knowing that he had to wait. Victoria was five feet, eight inches tall. She weighed about one hundred forty pounds, and had curves like a winding road. She had a dark caramel complexion and her lips were full. Her eyes were a beautiful shade of brown. When the sun hit them, they would change to a perfect honey brown, as if they were straight out of a honeycomb. Her father was African American and her mother was Spanish. She had her mother's grain of hair. Her full black hair was silky to the touch and always smelled like berries. Stuck in a small daze, checking out his wife while she basically told him that he missed his opportunity, Austin cut the conversation short. "Baby, baby. I have to go so I can get back to your fine ass," he said while grabbing Victoria and pulling her close as he slowly kisses her. "Mmm, baby you smell so good." Austin whispered in her ear. Victoria smiled and replied, "Thank you baby." He grips Victoria sides and back, kissing her from her lips to her chin then making his way to her neck. Moving his hands from her back to her waist, he pulls the towel off her and drops down to his knees to kiss her stomach. Things started to heat up and Austin felt like he had a second chance until his phone interrupted them "Ring, Ring" Bringing Victoria back to reality from her moment of passion. She stopped to grab the phone. "Austin?, umm baby... wait. You have so much to do. I'll be here when you get back, waiting on you with your favorite oils. But make sure you get everything done. I'll have something else special for you after the evening is over." Victoria promised. Looking up at Victoria, Austin asked, "Damn baby, can we just knock it out real quick and then we won't have to wait?" "No baby, you know I like to build things up and let you break them down." she replied, looking down at Austin and biting her bottom lip with a smile. Austin stood up while exhaling with frustration. Victoria hugged Austin and said, "I'm all yours when you get back." "Yeah, yeah. Whatever Vicky." Frustrated, Austin turned around and headed to the door, "Love you baby" he yelled with defeat in his voice. Victoria yelled back, "Bye, love you too." Austin slammed the door and walked to his truck. Looking around he could see a few of his neighbors. While some where cutting their yard and others were washing their cars, Austin waves saying, "Good morning." Pulling off he thought, "Damn, I should have stayed in bed. Now I don't feel like running any errands." After about fifteen to twenty minutes, Austin arrived at Thomas house calling him to come outside. In true Thomas fashion, he did not pick up the phone. Austin got out of his truck and walked to the door. As soon as Austin raised his hand to knock, Thomas was walking out saying, "Yo! I looked outside and you was headed to the door. I just had to use the bathroom real quick." Austin replied laughing, "You always have the bubble guts man. You need to go to the doctor for that." "Man whatever, let's just go." Thomas said as he slightly bumped Austin out of the way to shut the door. They both walked towards Austin's truck. "I can't believe you got me out the house, on a Sunday morning. It is nine A.M. I hope these errands are really important and not just you needing to hide from your wife." Thomas complained. "Yeah, they are. Damn! Quit sweating me man." Austin yelled as they both hopped in the truck. "Yeah, I'll drop it. But just to let you know. You are acting like a little bitch, hiding from your old lady." Thomas started laughing. "Yeah, whatever." Austin said as he thought to himself, "Maybe picking up Thomas was a bad idea after all." Thomas changed the conversation and asked "Where are we going to first?" "Well, I want to run to Lowe's first while it's still early. Before all the people get there." Thomas looked up and said "Austin, its Sunday. Who the hell you think is going to be in Lowe's this early in the morning?" "Contractors who are getting ready for their Monday and people who decided to do their yard work or whatever else today." Thomas sat in the truck as Austin drove with a silly look on his face and said, "Ok, you got me." Minutes later, they pulled up at Lowe's. Before getting out of the truck, Austin told Thomas his game plan was to get his pieces of wood and a few more grill appliances. Thomas agreed to be in and out, but Austin knew that he was taking a kid to a candy store. As they entered Lowe's, Thomas yelled, "Oh shit! That riding lawnmower is on sale. Yo A, I need that!" as he bolted over to the lawnmowers on display. "I can picture myself on this with a cold beer, headphones, and my shirt off cutting grass like I was in the matrix." Austin laughed and said, "Man come on, let's stick to the plan."

"Alright but you owe me. One morning we have to wake up early and you will come and help me get this heavy ass thing." "Yeah man, no problem. Let's just hurry up." Austin replied. They started to walk towards the back where the grills were. Thomas, feeling the pressure to hurry said, "Hey, why are you in so much of a rush?" "When I left the house Vicky was in her towel and said I could get that good shit when I get back." "Damn. Look at you. You know you're my boy and that I would never make a move on Vicky, but she fine as hell and to leave you high and dry like that in her towel... Shit, man I'll be rushing back home too." Thomas said as they came to the grill section of the store. "Yeah man I know right." Austin said agreeing with Thomas. "Yo, A? You know who I wouldn't mind have waiting at home for me?" "Who?" Austin replied. Thomas nodded his head, pointing towards a woman that was down the aisle, near the screen doors. Austin, turning his head to see who Thomas was talking about, almost instantly he agreed and said, "You damn right. I don't normally agree because I'm married, but she is fine. Are you going to say something to her?" "Yeah, but we have to come up with a game plan." "We?" Austin asked "Yes, we. You got me out here all early. That's the least you can do." Thomas replied. "Well, looks like I got you an opportunity since I called you this morning, and besides, 'we' are not going to be fucking her. You are. So stop being a... what was the words you use on me this morning? Oh, I know, 'a little bitch!' Gon' now." Austin said to Thomas as he laughed. "Man, come on. You my dog. My right hand man. Run me some wing man action." Thomas whined. Austin gave into Thomas and agreed. "Ok, I got you man. You fourtythree years old acting like a high school kid scared to talk to a woman." "Man shut up Austin. You just saying that because you're married. Who you think ran wing action when you met Vicky?" "Yeah, you keep talking to me like this and you won't have no wing action meeting this woman." Austin said. "Alright, quit playing. Come on let's go." Thomas said as his anxiousness was written all over his face. "I'm going to walk around the other side." "Yeah, yeah, alright. We looking like a small pack of old ass hyenas dividing and conquering its prey." Austin joked as they both laughed and set out on their mission. Austin made his way towards the woman. Thomas nervously walked to the other side trying to come up with a line to say as he mumbled to himself. Austin was checking out the beautiful woman as he made his way towards her. He knew he was married and could not say anything, but he could definitely look at her while Thomas tried his hand. This woman had a glowing champagne complexion. She was roughly five feet, six inches tall. He could tell she had a gym fit body by the way her leggings and shirt gripped her. This woman looks like she weighs about one hundred thirty-five pounds. She has cute dimples and as Austin got closer he realized that her eyes were grayish green. Her hair was in a ponytail and she had plain running shoes on. It was something intriguing about her and Austin couldn't wait to see how Thomas was going to blow this opportunity. Austin came close to the women and pulled out his phone as he greeted her. "Hello?" "Hi." The woman said. "You don't mind if I step in front of you to take some pictures do you? My wife was thinking about getting a new screen door." Austin asked. "Oh no, not at all. I'm actually waiting for a contractor to help me

14

find something nice for my house. I wanted to get here before all the other people got here. You know... other contractors and those who want to do there Sunday yard work." she said with a slight giggle. Austin turned around with a smirk and said, "Yeah, that's what I said." The women looked at Austin with a curious look on her face and asked, "You said what?" "I just told my friend the exact same thing about getting here before contractors and people doing yard work, but he didn't agree." The woman looked at Austin giggling as she was trying to figure out Austin's angle. Is he serious or is he trying to run game. Before she could respond, Thomas popped up from the other side of them. "Hey, there you are." The women instantly held her hand out to shake hands and said hi with a smile. "You must be Mr. Pitts. Good morning, I'm Cynthia Heights." Thomas agreed right away saying, "Yes, I am." Austin quickly corrected Thomas saying "No he's not. That's my close friend Thomas Clark, and I am Austin Roberts. This is my friend who came with me for support because I don't know where to start. I guess I didn't want to look stupid by myself." They all laughed. "Well I guess that makes three of us huh?" Cynthia said to Austin as they exchanged eye contact. Austin smiled and said, "Yeah, I guess it does." Thomas started to pick up on the vibe between Cynthia and Austin. Even though Austin was a faithful man, Thomas felt a little threaten and decided to cut their conversation short. "Austin, what kind of door does your wife want?" "What?" Austin asked Thomas as he was checking Cynthia out. "The door... your wife... what design?" Thomas replied, trying to snap Austin out of his daze. Austin turned around, clearing his throat and stumbling

15

over his words. "Ha, umm...I don't know. I'll take some pictures to show her." Thomas now had the floor. "So Cynthia, why are you here so early?" Austin looked at Cynthia as she looked back and chuckled. She realized that Thomas was the friend Austin was talking about earlier. Before she could answer, her phone rang. "Give me a sec." She told Thomas. Cynthia answered her phone and walked off. Meanwhile, Thomas asked Austin, "Man, what's up with that?" "What's up with what?" "I mean, you and her all giggly and shit. She acting like she checking for you." Thomas replied. "Nah man. She not checking for me and besides I'm married fool." "Yeah, well shit, you're cock blocking me like I'm married." Thomas fired back. "I'm not doing shit. What you talking about T?" "Man she was trying to make eye contact with you." "Trying? Her fine ass was." Austin teased while laughing at his friend. "See, that's what I'm saying. You're blocking because you can't have her." "Look man, I'm going to back off but you need to hurry up. My baby waiting on me at home." Austin said, reminding him that this was supposed to be an in and out thing. "How the hell are you going to block me then put me on a time limit? Man, I need to find a new friend." Austin smiled at Thomas and said, "Well, there you are. You can start with Cynthia because she's on her way back. Hey, and don't forget, tick tock, tick tock." Said Austin as he walked away. Cynthia walked up and asked, "Hey, where did Austin go?" "His wife texted him about some lights or something." Thomas lied trying to reiterate that Austin was married. "Oh, ok. Well, it was nice meeting you. My contractor just canceled on me so I'm about to leave." she said with disappointment in her voice. Thomas couldn't tell if she was disappointed about her contractor or the fact that Austin was gone. He tried a little damage control. "Oh, that sucks. So why do you have a contractor anyway? You don't have a man to help you with all this man stuff?" "That was cute but I don't have one because I'm single and I just transferred to a new company." Cynthia was being cautious because she realized she gave too much information away. She quickly added, "And my brother's at work." "I understand that. That's wonderful. New place, new opportunity. It's like you have a new life. Feels kind of free huh?" Thomas asked. "Yeah, I guess you can say that." She replied. "Well I'm pretty sure Austin is done shopping. You mind if I walk you out?" Cynthia took a quick second look at Thomas. Checking out his broad shoulders, his posture, and physique. Thomas was a very handsome dark skin man. He had a head full of hair that he kept cut, neat and low. He stood six feet one inch tall, about two hundred and twenty pounds and had a chiseled chin with a very attractive smile that was complimented by egg shell white teeth. He had tattoos on his arms that fit well with his muscular physique. "Sure, I don't mind. It's Thomas right?" "Yeah, it's Thomas. Cynthia right?" he asked, even though he had not forgotten her name. "Yes, my name is Cynthia." She replied coyly, knowing that Thomas knew her name. "So how long has Austin been married?" Cynthia asked, as they were walking towards the exit. "I'll say about twenty years. Why? Are you checking for him or something? I mean shouldn't you be talking to him and not me?" Thomas asked with a hint a jealousy in his voice. "What's that supposed to mean?" Cynthia asked. "I'm just saying. I was trying to holla but it seems like you're into married

17

men. Maybe I should go get married and then try my hand." Cynthia stopped dead in her tracks. She looked at Thomas and said, "How dare you talk to me like I'm some kind of hoe or slut that's in the streets messing up happy homes? My husband cheated on me and I wouldn't want any women going through the pain and heartbreak that I did. The reason I asked you how long your friend has been married, was to see how long he'd been teaching you to be a better man. See, men that settle down and are faithful, show men like yourself how to be grounded. Everybody loves new gifts, pets, and flings. People just love new everything because it new. But when you can take something new and learn to treasure it as it gets older, you start to understand the value of that treasure. Now Thomas, I think you have played around so much that you forgot where you placed your map and now you have lost a treasure baby..." Cutting her off Thomas replied, "Calm down. I'm sorry. I really didn't mean it like that." Cynthia looked at Thomas even harder as if she could see through him and asked, "Well how did you mean it?" Thomas looked at Cynthia with a blank face. Cynthia took a deep breath and relaxed the tension in her face as her eyes widen and said, "I thought so" and walked off from him, exiting the store. Austin was sitting in his truck browsing the internet on his phone when he happened to look up and see Cynthia leaving out the store. He noticed that she was walking fast and figured she was in a rush. As she walked across the parking lot, Austin tapped the horn and waved. Cynthia turned and saw it was Austin. She headed towards his truck and asked, "Austin, right?" "Yeah, that's right." Austin said with a smile. "Well, let me tell you something Austin. I

18

haven't known you no more than 30 minutes tops, but I had taken notice in you and what I've seen so far is that you are a very polite man. Seems like you are a very incredible husband that treasures his wife." "I do." Austin said as Cynthia continued, "You are very attractive and I'm sure you have a great personality." Austin lowered his eyebrow and slightly tilted his head. He asked, "I don't mean to be rude, but where are you going with this?" She broke eye contact by looking down at ground to hide her pain. Gathering herself, Cynthia looked up at Austin and replied, "I'm just simply saying, us women need more faithful and respectful men like you." As soon as Cynthia mentioned respectful men like him, Austin said to himself, "Aww shit! What the hell did Thomas say?" Austin calmly said, "Thank you. Not trying to overstep my boundaries but you are very attractive yourself and I believe without a doubt in my mind you will find someone who loves you as much as I love my wife." Cynthia smiled softly and said, "Thank you." as she thought to herself, "Damn, why are the good ones always taken?" She looked up to her left and saw that Thomas was heading back to the truck. She didn't want to talk to Thomas so she turned to Austin and quickly said, "Bye stranger. It was nice meeting you." with seduction in her voice as she walked away. Austin sat there and watched the sway in her hips as she headed to her car. Breaking his gaze, Thomas hopped in the truck and said, "Aww, that's sweet. She came to say bye." "Shut up, Thomas. And what the hell you say to her anyways. I knew you were going to be ignorant and mess it up. I should have stayed." Austin yelled. Still a little jealous, Thomas mumbled, "Maybe you should have stayed then." while jerking his head. "You are going to be dipping and dabbing forever man. You are getting old. Those young girls that let you fill their heads up with nonsense not going be around much longer." Austin said while laughing. "Man, stop tripping on me. Don't be mad at me because I came to the truck. Y'all could have still played Romeo and Juliet at her car." "Yeah whatever. So what you say to her?" Thomas leaned back in the seat, looking out the window with a stupid look on his face and guilt written all over him. Austin loudly shouted, "Spit it out fool!" "I just said, maybe she wanted a married man. Shit, how she was checking you out, you probably could have gotten both us to fuck her." Austin shook his head as he started the truck. Looking at Thomas he said, "You stupid as hell, you know that?" "I mean, how I was supposed to know she got cheated on." Thomas confessed. "Hold on. You basically told a woman who had heart broken, who had her home wrecked, that maybe she wants a man that's married so she can be the one that creep and break up a home." Austin pulled up to a red light, looked at Thomas, and stared at him with a blank face. After a few seconds Thomas yelled, "What!? What you looking at?" Being very sarcastic Austin replied, "I'm looking at my best friend Thomas, the fucking genius. You are just a genius." Thomas then asked, "How was I supposed to know?" shrugging his shoulder. Austin said, "How about, first, you be nice, then you have a nice conversation about something. Then you ask a nice question that may lead to a bad answer. Questions like, have you ever been married? Maybe you would get answers like, 'Yes, but he won't shit and he cheated on me.' You been around me for a long time Thomas and I still have to teach you shit."

Austin said as he laughed. Thomas looked over at Austin. Suddenly fearing that he was going to be old and alone, he played it safe by changing the conversation. "I'm just going to keep pimping. Maybe I'll just marry one of my hoes." Thomas joked. "Maybe. Love is love." Austin said shaking his head in disappointment. "Speaking of love, I missed my love's phone call messing around with you... Mr. Pimp of the Year." "See, she left you a voicemail. She probably wanted you to go run all her errands and see, a guy like me don't have women calling and telling me to do things. I tell them. It's like a lion thing. You know, king of the jungle. Probably something you don't know about." While Thomas was running off at the mouth about nothing, Austin was checking his voicemail, only to hear Vicky say, "Hurry up." Trying to figure out what Vicky was talking about, he then heard a man's voice say, "What? Do you think we're going to get caught? Austin has no idea." Then Vicky agreed and said, "You're right, but I don't want him to catch you here because it's definitely going to be hell to pay." In shock, Austin pulls the truck over. Thomas looked over at Austin. "Hey man, you ok?" he asked. Austin sat in the truck quiet and still staring off in a daze. Thomas asked again, "Austin, you ok? What's wrong? What happened?" Austin still didn't reply. Thomas yelled, "Yo!" Austin turned and looked at Thomas while putting his phone on speaker. Thomas listened and asked, "How long ago did Vicky send the message? The guy might be still there." Austin looked at Thomas as if he was right and said, "I just missed the call." Then without hesitation, he smashed on the gas. His tires screamed as rubber melted on the pavement leaving a trail of tire marks behind him. Rushing in and out traffic,

Thomas instigated the situation by saying, "That's fucked up man. How long you think Vicky been cheating? If they at your crib now, how many times you think they fucked in your bed? Yo, what if dude have like, a 12-inch dick or something?" Before Thomas could get another word out Austin yelled, "Shut the fuck up! I'm thinking. I don't need your crazy ass comments or ideas right now." They got closer to the house and they both noticed a truck was parked in the driveway. Thomas yelled "Aww hell no. And this nigga parked in your driveway." Pissed off, but extremely hurt, Austin once again reminded Thomas that he needed to shut up. He slowly pulled up at the house, parking in front of a neighbor's house so his truck would not be seen. Austin told Thomas that he was going to go around the back to look through the back sliding door. Austin instructed Thomas to stay in the front of the house and yell if someone comes out. They both agreed on the plan and hopped out of the truck. Austin ran around to the back of his house, looking in every window that he could before reaching the sliding door. As he walked up, he could hear voices talking and laughing. Then he peeped in the sliding door and saw Vicky hugging a man. Then she stopped and said, "Ok, I have to give it to you. You're the man. Everything was perfect but you must leave, like right now." Austin became extremely mad. His eyes filled with rage as he stormed around to the front of the house. As he was walking, he heard Thomas yell, "Austin, Austin! Its mother fucking Drew!" Andrew is Vicky's best friend, Michelle's, husband. Austin then stood there looking at Drew and asked, "So you fucking my wife? What do you think Michelle would think about all this?" Drew looked at Vicky then looked at Austin and

22

said, "Austin, what are you talking about?" as he shrugged his shoulders. "Drew, you think this is a fucking game? I just seen you hugging all up on Vicky!" Austin yelled. Vicky cut Austin off and said, "No baby you're…" but before she could finish her sentence, Austin said, "Look Vicky, you see men talking. Go inside the house and I'll deal with your ass when I'm done kicking his." Vicky replied, "You don't know what you're talking about. Baby calm down." Before Austin could respond, another guy came out of the front door. Thomas yelled, "Aww hell no! Fuck this talking shit Austin. Somebody have to go!" "What the fuck is this shit? You fucking niggas in my house, the house that I paid for?" Austin snapped, rushing towards Drew with Thomas right behind him. But before he could get to Drew, Vicky yelled at Andrew and the other guy to get in the house as she shut the door. Vicky started screaming at Austin. "What the hell is wrong with you!? I am not cheating on you" as she pushed him. "I fucking heard you Vicky, I heard it all! 'Hurry up before he comes back.'" Austin yelled as they locked eyes. Austin's were filled with rage. "Drew supposed to be like family and y'all creeping." "Wait." Vicky said with relief in her voice. "Andrew was bringing over the TV I had brought for you. I was going to surprise you. That's why he's here. They had it at their house. I was waiting for the right moment to bring it over here dumbass!" "What? A TV?" he said as he put his hands on this head and looking at Vicky as if he knew was wrong. Austin then looked back at Thomas with embarrassment all on his face. Thomas raised his eyebrows looking down at the ground. Austin turned and looked at Vicky. She had her mouth twisted up and yelled, "You just embarrassed me in front of the whole neighborhood!" Austin began to feel relieved, until he thought about how Vicky was going to kill him. She turned and walked in the house while calling Austin a stupid asshole. Austin was on Vicky's heels as he yelled, "Baby, I'm sorry. How do you think I was supposed to act?" Thomas made his way in the house and went straight to the living room. Thomas saw Andrew and the other guy and slightly nodded his head. "Whelp Drew, you would have done the same thing if your partner behind you would have been with you too." Andrew said, "Yeah you're right. Shit, I never seen Austin mad. I was confused." Then Thomas laughed and said, "We know who ain't getting no ass for the next month." The guys laughed, and Thomas made his way to the kitchen to grab some beers. They made themselves comfortable and looked at the 80-inch curved TV. "That's a nice ass TV." Thomas said. Agreeing with him Andrew replied, "That's what I said. I wish Michelle would buy me an 80-inch TV. Hell, I wish her ass would buy me lunch." They all laughed. In the mist of them laughing Austin walked in and said, "Look Drew, I'm sorry man. I really apologize, I know you wouldn't disrespect. I'll talk to you later today at the cookout. But right now, since y'all are being buddy, buddy and I have Vicky pissed off, I'm going to need y'all to buddy y'all asses out and go home." Thomas said, "But I rode with you." "Yeah, I know. Now ride with your new buddies." "Man, it's always something." Thomas mumbled. "Yeah, yeah." Austin said as he led them to the door. Andrew was the last to leave and Austin pulled him to the side and said, "Look man..." Drew cut Austin off and said, "I get it. Chill Austin." Austin gave Drew a hand shake with a hug and asked, "You still coming to the cookout right?" Drew laughed and replied, "Yeah man I'll be here ready to eat and get drunk." "My man." Austin said as Andrew left. Austin shut the front door and walk towards the bedroom where Vicky was sitting on the bed. She had the most pissed off look on her face that he has ever seen, in all the years they had been married. As soon as Austin hit the doorway Vicky yelled, "How dare you accuse me of cheating on you! And out of all places, our house, Austin! I can't believe you! I love you and you accuse me of cheating on you." Austin said, "Baby I'm sorry. Here baby, listen to this." She listened to the voicemail and said, "You still should have asked instead of acting a fool." In a softer tone, Vicky said, "You were all mad and passionate looking, had me all fired up about how mad and aggressive you were. I loved how you put me in my place. What did you say baby? 'You're going to deal with my ass after you kick his?' " Vicky said as she lowered her hand to rub her thighs. While biting her lip, she smiled. Then she laid on the bed and asked, "Are you going to come use that aggressiveness on me now?" Austin didn't waste any time taking his clothes off as he made his way to Vicky. She laid there thinking to herself how cute Austin looked. He finally made it to the bed, hopping on his beautiful wife with a springing erection preparing to slip right inside her. Vicky kissed Austin as she began to get wet. They both tugged and pulled at each other. The foreplay was soon over after Vicky whispered softly to Austin, "Get inside me." Austin passed the lips of Vicky's core while they tightly attach around the thickness of his shaft. Entering inside her, he began feeling the flow of her juices. "I love you baby." Vicky said holding on tight to

25

Austin. "I love you too." Austin said rolling over to putting Vicky on top off him. Vicky worked her hips, riding Austin as her juices creamed up. Holding on to Vicky, he felt her body starting to tense as he grabbed her closer. Kissing her on her neck and squeezing Vicky's nipples, he told her, "Cum for me baby. I want you to cum on this dick." Vicky moaned louder. "I'ma cum for you baby! I'ma cum!" she said while reaching her climax as Austin reached his. Looking at each other, they both smiled with a sexual satisfaction. "That was a great quickie! That was amazing baby." Vicky said breathlessly. Austin agreed. Vicky rolled off Austin as they laid side by side, looking at the ceiling they both dozed off fast asleep.

Chapter 2.

Austin opened his eyes and looked at the clock. It was only a few hours before the cookout was to start. "Vicky, wake up, wake up! We don't have long until the cookout starts. Get up Vicky!" he yelled. "Alright, what time is it?" Vicky asked. "Its 2:43" "Are you serious?" Vicky asked closing her eyes she exhaled, realizing she was running behind. Austin finally made it to the kitchen and began sorting out the food and preparing things for the cookout when he heard keys at the door. Curious, he walked to the door to see who was there. As the door opened he heard, "Hey daddy!" Jasmine shouted. "Hey baby girl" Austin said hugging Jasmine. "What are you doing here so early?" "Well, I figured you and mom would need my help so I came early". "Thanks Jas, glad you did because we just woke up." "Just woke up?" Jasmine said with a low tone in her voice. "Why are y'all just waking up? You and mom knew about this cookout yesterday" "Yeah, well your mom and I had to take care of some business, if you know what I mean" "That's nasty daddy, I didn't need to know that at all." Austin laughed as he started sorting the food and doing a little two step. "All I'm saying, baby girl, is that we like to get our freak on too." "Momma!" Jasmine yelled walking down the hallway. "Daddy telling me about y'all sex life again. Make him stop." Surprised and excited to hear Jasmine's voice, Vicky paid no mind to what Jasmine was talking about. "Hey baby." She said, hugging Jasmine with a smile. "What are you doing here so early? You know the cookout doesn't start for another two hours or so." "I

27

know. I thought I'd come and help out." Jasmine responded. "That's great. We are running late anyway." "I know. Dad told me all about you and him being grown." "Well baby, he didn't lie. He put me to bed if you know what I mean." Jasmine looked at Vicky with a steel face. "Mom, that's nasty. I don't want to hear anything about you and dad ever again." Still smiling, Vicky said, "Baby, if it's the truth then let it shine in the light." "No, that's the dark. The thought of you and dad naked is dark and should be kept between you, him, and the darkness." Still holding her smile Vicky said, "I need you to sort the food. I know your lazy ass daddy is going to try and do that instead of taking them chairs out." Laughing, Jasmine agreed and said, "He already started sorting the food." "That lazy ass man." Vicky said shaking her head. "Oh, so now he's lazy?" Vicky looked at Jasmine and asked. "You want me to tell you some more sparkling details about me and your daddy?" "Ok, ok. I'm going to go sort the food." "That's what I thought." Vicky said. Jasmine began making her way to the hallway when she seen Austin sorting the food and said, "I'll take it from her pops. Mom wants you to take the chairs out and set them up." "That damn woman always wants things done her way." Austin fussed, as Jasmine laughed. "I guess I'll go and knock it out." Austin said frustrated. The doorbell rang as he headed outside. "I'll get it Daddy. It's probably Patrick. I told him to meet me here." "Oh, you did huh!?" Austin replied. "Yeah, what's the problem?" Jasmine asked looking curious. "Oh nah, nothing. I was just wondering why he had to meet you. Why you and Patrick didn't ride together?" He asked with suspicion all in his voice. "Oh, you acting like you was holding out or had something you wanted to say." She said. Walking in the kitchen, cutting in the conversation, Vicky asked, "Who wanted to say what?" Jasmine responded, "Dad was acting funny because I mentioned Patrick at the door." Victory replied, "Funny? Jasmine, you know your dad acts funny towards everyone." "Yeah, I know." When Jasmine walked off, Vicky said, "Austin, you better act right and don't you blow the surprise for her." "I'm not going to blow nothing." Austin said as he shut the door on Vicky. Patrick then walked in. "Hey. How are you Mrs. V? "Hey Patrick. I'm good. How's that hospital treating you?" "So far so good Mrs. V. I'm shooting to get the job at my friend's practice so I can have a little more time for your daughter. If I get the job, I won't be on call as much." Patrick explained. "Do what you have to do to take care of my baby girl. Just keep faith and it will all work out." Vicky said as she winked her eye. "You're right Mrs. V. With faith, things always workout." "Hey baby," Jasmine chimed in, "my dad is outside and I'm pretty sure he's going to need your help." Yeah no problem." Patrick said as he made his way out the door. "Hey, what's up Mr. Roberts? How you doing today?" "What's up Patrick? I was doing great before these heavy ass chairs was put in my plans." "Oh, I'll get them for you." Patrick said, grabbing a pair of chairs. Austin thought to himself. "Who does Patrick think he's fooling? He think he's slick, trying to kiss my ass." But he didn't refuse the help. "Thanks, Patrick. You can grab them tables while you're at it." "Yeah, sure I'll get them." Patrick said. While Austin was planning on enjoying Patrick kissing up to him, he heard, "Yo! Yo!" He looked back and there was Thomas. "Perfect." Austin thought as he made his way to Thomas.

"What's up, T." "Nothing much," Thomas replied. He continues while laughing, "You good from this morning? Vicky didn't kick your ass did she?" "Nah, nah man. I put it down and she forgave me. You know how that go." Austin bragged. "Oh yeah. This one girl tried to be all mad at me. I hit her with the happy dick and she haven't been mad ever sense." "You a fucking lie." Austin said as they both laughed. Taking notice of Patrick, Thomas said, "I see you putting doctor boy to work." "Yeah, I am." Austin said. "Yeah, you need to make him tough with his punk ass." Thomas replied. Austin looked at Thomas and asked, "Why you always giving him a hard time?" "What you mean?" Thomas asked. "I'm just saying. You give the kid a hard time. You just always down talking him. Is it hard for you to understand the boy went to school, busted his ass and made something of himself? Let him be." He told Thomas. "Woah, woah. Why are you so touchy about him today? What's up with that?" "Nothing man." Austin said. "Nah, it's something. You putting him on a pedestal and a high one at that." Austin looked at Thomas and said. "You better not say shit." With a curious but nervous look Thomas said, "I'm not. What's up?" Austin Continued, "Look man, if I tell you and you say anything, I'll kick your ass myself." "Man, I'm not going to say anything. What's up?" Thomas said rushing to hear the news. "Alright man, don't say shit. I know you Thomas," "Just tell me already." Austin then whispered, "Patrick is going to ask for my permission to marry Jas." "What?!" Thomas said loudly. "Lower your damn voice." Austin said as Patrick looked over at them. "You not going to say yes, are you?" Thomas asked. "I wasn't really feeling the kid when I first met him. But he turned out to

30

be a good guy. He made me some promises, kept his word and worked things out. So yeah, I'm going to give him the green light." "Twisting up his face and looking at Patrick as he was putting out the chairs, Thomas said, "The green light." "Yeah, what's wrong? You don't want your god-daughter having the best?" "Yeah, but I'm just saying. They only been dating a few years and they're still young." "Thomas, do you hear yourself right now? You didn't say any of that when Vicky and I got married at 24 years old." "Yeah, I know. But this guy?" "Yes, that guy. He's family now. So, cut the bullshit and let's help him set up these damn tables." "Alright, you're right. Let's help him." Thomas said raising his hands and eyebrows. As they walked over to help Patrick, Austin wondered why Thomas was acting so weird. He decided not to pay it any mind. "What's up Thomas?" Patrick asked. Glimpsing at Austin for a quick second, Thomas said. "Ain't nothing young buck. Thought I'd come and get a beer early, but I guess I'll have to help out like you." They all laughed, and Patrick said. "Don't worry. I think I have something for you later. The good stuff." "That's what I like to hear." Thomas said. Then Austin butted in the conversation." How about we get this done so we can get to the good stuff faster." "I agree." Patrick responded as they continued to put the table and chairs out. An hour or so past and all the chairs, tables, and candles were nice, neat and in place for the cookout. The men headed into the house hoping to get some food for their hard work, but Vicky shut that down. "Why every year do you and Thomas, try to come and eat before the cookout starts?" "Why do you try and stop us every year? You know damn well we was coming to get some food, but you're trying to play goalie and protect it." Instigating the conversation, Thomas said, "Yeah, why?" "Vicky shouted, "Thomas, you shut up. And it's a cookout. You eat when the others get here. And the most important reason is, y'all are sweaty and y'all dirty asses never even washed your hands." "I washed mine Mrs. V." Patrick said, drying off his hands. "Oh, you did?" Vicky asked. "Well gone and fix you something." Austin looked at Patrick and said, "If you eat before me in my house, I'm going to kick your little ass." Patrick immediately stopped walking towards the food with fear written all on his face. Vicky fired back, "Remember all that talk you was telling Jasmine about, playing around before everyone got here?" Austin looked at Vicky and frowned as he answered. "Yes." Vicky then raise her right eyebrow and said, "That will be your last time talking about it for a while if he don't eat before you." Austin balled his face up. "I'll wash my hands and make him a plate." Thomas looked confuse and walk off with Austin saying, "Now see, that's what I'm talking about. You let Vicky talk to you any ole kind of way. Now you fixing this boy your plate." "Shut up Thomas. You don't get it. That's why your ass is single now. See, Vicky can feel like she in control all she wants. But she's not." Still confused, Thomas asked, "What you mean Austin?" "See, that's like my time to shine. When she thinks she checking me. Understand, it doesn't bother me because I'm going to get everything I want. I'm going to fix this little punk a plate... along with mine. I still eat before the cookout. Vicky still think she has the upper hand of whatever woman world she thinks she rules. Last but not least is, I'm still going to get the ass without dealing with her bullshit." Laughing, Thomas said. "That would have been my main focus." Austin shook his head. "Thomas, that's why you can't get anything in order with your life. You just think about ass all day. That's called not having dick control." "I have dick control." Thomas replied. "No you don't. You run around with your dick out all day. The women don't even have to wait. Shit, they get the sex from you and dipped. The only one getting played is yourself. You chasing them. All while they're getting what they want and continuing to chase their dream and future careers. Meanwhile, you're bullshitting. You are going to in up alone when you're happy stick stops working." Austin said while laughing. "Now let me wash my hands and mastermind this woman's game plan. I would say, 'You know what I mean,' but you don't." Austin then walked in the bathroom to wash his hands as Thomas stood there knowing Austin was right. Thomas made his way back to the kitchen to wash his hands. Vicky said, "You and Austin better not be in the bathroom together washing your hands and giggling like two school boys." "Nah Vicky. We two grown men." Thomas said smiling at Vicky. "Yeah right. You and my husband are far from grown men." They both started laughing. Thomas then put on a serious face and asked. "You think Patrick is grown enough for marriage?" Vicky eyes got big as she looked around to see where Jasmine was. Gladly, Jasmine was nowhere in sight. "I know Austin couldn't keep his damn mouth close! You didn't say anything?" Vicky asked Thomas. "No, I'm not either. Don't be mad at Austin. Jasmine is his only girl and I'm his best friend. Who else is he was going to talk to about this whole thing. You knew I was going to find out right when I walk in. I'm happy for them. I just want to have the best for my god-daughter." Thomas explain. "Well I guess you're right." Vicky said with relief. "I know. I just have to make sure he's the right guy is all I'm saying. If I was a young doctor around all them young nurses, it would sure be hard for me being married and having them around." Thomas said trying to convince Vicky. "Yeah, you right. It would be hard for you, but Jasmine not marrying you, Thomas. Honestly, having you around makes me see how grateful I am to see that my daughter is not getting played. You know, not having her mind and body broke down like you do women. Now I know you love her and want the best for her. But do see that Patrick's heart is not like yours. You wouldn't understand to see the difference. Thomas, I love you like you're my own brother. I don't want you to take nothing I say wrong, but it's best to look in the mirror and start to see your faults instead of trying to point out others. Before you try and point fingers at Patrick, really think how he's not like you. Now come on Thomas. Guest will be arriving soon. Can you go put the charcoal in the grill and wrap the foil around the racks?" Vicky asked trying to change the vibe. Thomas looked at Vicky as she smirked. Then he turned and grabbed some forks and spoons to sit on the tables. "Sure thing." Thomas replied, holding in his comments as he walked outside. About an hour later. The doorbell sounded with the first guest. Moments later, more family and friends started to pack the cookout. Things were going well and everyone was enjoying themselves. Patrick walked up to Austin. "Mr. Roberts. Can I talk to you for a second?" Austin looked at Patrick with a grin and asked. "Sure. What's this about?" as if he didn't already know. "It's about my future." He answered as they walked from the crowd. "Oh yeah. How so?" "Well Mr. Roberts. I know when we first met, I wasn't the man you wanted to date your daughter. I dropped out of med school..." "No, you were forced out of school because you were selling drugs." "Drugs that are now legal in some states, and my charges were dropped." Patrick said feeling as if he was losing the conversation early. "I was selling drugs to get through school, but that's not me anymore" "Son, your charges were dropped because of a bad cop who got caught doing bad things before your court date. Other than that, you would have been in the pen right now serving five to seven years." "Mr. Roberts, can't you see I understand that? I saw what road I was going down and changed paths. I have a legit career. I'm a fucking doctor. I've change my ways from being about short cuts and learned how to work hard. I'm a great guy who respects you and your family. Mr. Roberts, I am..." Before Patrick could finish Austin cut him off. "Stop, I know Patrick. I know how you've changed. I know how you looked me in my eye and begged for my permission to let you call my daughter. You know I trust you." "But Mr. Roberts." said Patrick, trying to talk over Austin. "Didn't I say stop, Patrick!" Austin shouted. "You promised me and told me that you would show me that you deserved my daughter. I surely hope you're not this nervous when you asking Jasmine to marry you?" "Austin started laughing as Patrick looked at him in shocked. Relieved, Patrick asked, "You knew this whole time?" "I know everything. I also have a wife with a big mouth." Patrick hands started shaking as he fought his tears from falling. Patrick stuck his chest out, looked Austin in his eyes and said. "Mr. Austin Roberts. Would you give me the honor and allow

35

me to ask your daughter for her hand in marriage?" Austin looked at Patrick and said, "Yes." Patrick rushed Austin, hugging him while saying, "I won't let you down." Austin stood there with his hands still in the air. He didn't know if he should hug Patrick back or not. He glanced towards the front door where Thomas stood. Thomas, with a smile, nodded his head towards Austin as if he had just done the right thing. As Thomas walked from the door, Austin said to Patrick, "Ok, ok. Stop with all this emotional stuff before I change my mind. I know you don't want me thinking my little girl is marrying a girl." Patrick quickly release Austin and said. "Yeah you're right." Drying his teary eyes, he got himself together as he made his way back around the side of the house. Austin headed to the porch, sat down on the stairs and began drinking his beer. He felt happy to be in his shoes and was glad that he made his choice. A few minutes later, Austin noticed Michelle and Andrew making their way up the drive way. Andrew said, "Call the owners. Their guard dog is loose again." They both laughed as Austin apologize once more and gave each other fives. "Yeah, I told you Austin, it's all good. I would have done the same thing." Michelle butted in and said. "No he wouldn't have. He would have been glad to pass me along so he could look at sports center and not be bothered." "Damn, I didn't think of that" Austin said as they all laughed." Well, what are you doing out here by yourself?" Michelle asked. "I'm just getting some air. Not drunk enough to deal with all these people." "I understand that" Andrew said. "Well, let's head back so I can get to that point." Austin suggested. They laughed as they made their way to the back yard. "Vicky, look who I found wondering the wild streets." Vicky smiled and said, "If it's not my best friend in the whole world." "Yeah, I'm your best friend and I know when you say that it only means one thing. So what is it?" Michelle asked as she laughed. Vicky struggled to hold her smile in and said. "Well girl, you do know me. Let's go in the house. I have to show you this dress and these shoes I got on sale last week." "I knew it. I knew it." Michelle said while laughing. The women walked off and made their way into the house. Andrew and Austin grabbed some beers and made their way to the fellas. "What up? What up?" Andrew said as he gave the fellas a five. Brad, a close friend of the family that works with Vicky, said, "Nothing much. I was just telling everyone about our new hires at the job. I mean, damn, these bitches are bad. All of them are from out of state. Make me want to leave and move to find me a wife." They all laughed. Brad continued, "Thomas, I know you still pimping like always." "Yeah, I am. But I'm getting too old. I may have to leave it up to you young boys, man." Patrick said, "Thomas, your stroke game getting bad huh." They laughed and Thomas said "Only if you knew." With a smile on his face. "I maybe old, but I'm an old man with working hips." They all look at each other and said. "It's all in the hips." Then the fellas laughed once more. Patrick's pager went off. "Well guys, it's been great! Duty calls. I'll see you later Mr. Roberts. Make sure you guys don't let me see you in the ER for drinking and driving." Thomas replied, "Aww go ahead man. We are grown men." Patrick said, "Ok, I'm serious. Y'all be good." As he walked away, he let Jasmine know that he had to leave. Thomas stood right next to Austin as Patrick walked off and whispered, "So that's what he do? Just up and leave when the pager goes off? Wonder when that will become an excuse to just leave the house late." Austin pulled Thomas to the side. "What the hell is your problem? You're steady trying to convince me that Patrick is a big cheater like you. Why? All day when he comes near you, you get up tight as if you haven't known this boy for years. What's the problem? If it's something I need to know, you need to spit it out. If it's nothing, drop it and be happy for your god-daughter and her future husband." Thomas looked Austin in the eyes and said. "It's nothing. You told me to have your back. You told me to make sure when things and events like this happen, make sure you are one hundred percent sure. Do you remember that?" Austin's body language changed, showing relief. Looking at the ground then looking back up to Thomas, Austin smiled and said, "Yeah, I asked you that right before I made you Jasmine's God-dad." Austin chuckled and said. "What was it? If Jasmine about to get married test me and my family to make sure we are not blinded by our happiness and love." Thomas smiled and said. "Well, I think Patrick is your new son in-law." Austin stuck his hand out as Thomas proudly gave his friend a five. Then pulled him in for a hug. "We help and we forgive to stay strong together." Thomas said, remembering a pack that the two friends use to say. Before they could release from their hug. Vicky came up and said in a joking manner, "Aww, that's sweet. Two grown emotional men." Then she laughed. Austin and Thomas quickly released each other. "Yeah, whatever Vicky." Austin said. Vicky looked at Austin, but before she walked off, she said, "Baby, its ok. I won't tell Thomas you cried before we had sex. Men can be emotional too."

Thomas eyes opened wide. "What! Austin, you cried during sex!" Then busted out laughing. Austin rushed off behind Vicky, looking back at Thomas saying, "Man, don't believe that shit!" Thomas walked behind Austin laughing, asking Vicky, "Was it a full blown cry or sensitive drops? I need to know this." Thomas said, laughing still. Austin stopped Thomas in his tracks and said, "Hey, Vicky was lying. Don't you go over there telling them lies on me." Thomas stood in front of Austin trying his best not to laugh in Austin's face. "Thomas, I'm serious man." Austin said as Thomas continued to try not to crack a smile. "I'm going to get me a fresh drink." Austin said as he headed inside the house. He ran into Jasmine who was looking all over the tables. "What are you doing baby girl?" Jasmine stopped what she was doing. "Daddy, I can't find my keys. I'm not sure where they are and the last person who had them was Patrick but he left for surgery and he won't be back until late." "Well Jasmine. If anything, you can stay here." "No dad, I have a board meeting in the morning that I can't be late for." "Ok Jasmine, someone will take you home". Andrew walked in the house as Jasmine said okay, still on the hunt for her keys. "Hey Austin? You have any more dogs left to throw on the grill? These drunk clowns are definitely going to need some more food to feed that liquor." "Yeah, sure. Looking in the fridge and Austin grab them." "Hey, you want a fresh cold one?" Austin asked. "Yeah, why not. I'll double fist it." Andrew said. "Hold on man. We had a rough start to our day and I haven't apologized in the right way. Look in that bottom cabinet and hand me that brown bag." Andrew did just that. Austin grabbed the bag out of Andrew's hand and pulled out a bottle of

Johnny Walker Green Label. Andrew's eyes lit up like firework on the 4th. "That's the green label. The green label is aged 15 years." "Yep." Austin replied. Then he grabbed two glasses and poured the drinks. He passed Andrew a glass and said, "To good friendship." "To good friendship." Andrew said, accepting the toast. The men took a sip of the 15 year old scotch and walked to the back yard. They made their way back to the group of men. Brad called out to Austin. "Hey, you know what my college girlfriend did when I told her I love her? Austin asked, "Did she run away?" "No she got emotional and cried during sex." The men burst out laughing, as Austin looked at Thomas. Thomas then bumped Austin and said, "Cheer up. We know it was a joke." Austin finally smiled and said, "Well Thomas cries all emotional too." The guys looked at Thomas and asked, "When?" Smiling, Austin looked back over his shoulder to see if Vicky was near. He then turned back around and said, "Back in college, when Serena Royal told her friends his dick was small." Everyone starting laughing as Thomas was fumbling his words to explain what happened. Before he could get anything out Jasmine walked up and said, "Daddy, I need to go soon. Can you take me home in 10 minutes?" Thomas butted in, "What's wrong with your car?" "I misplace my car keys. Good thing I have a spare to my house here." "Well, how you going to get in your car?" Thomas asked. "Umm, I have a spare in my house." I just need to go there and come back here." "Well, I'll take you. We can go now. I need to run to the store anyway for some Newport's." "Ok, cool. I'll gather my things and wait in the front." Jasmine said with a smile on her face. Austin said, "Thomas, you don't have to do that. I can

40

take her." Thomas said, "It's no problem. Besides, I said I was going to the store. No need for both of us to leave. Trust me. I'm not going to say anything." "Yeah, you're right. Well if you don't come back I'll see you tomorrow." Thomas look at Austin and said, "I'm coming back." "Man, I know you. It's getting late and you already have a to-go plate." Thomas laughed and said, "Yeah, you're right. I'll see you clowns later this week." They all gave Thomas a five as he left to take Jasmine home. Time passed as the crowd died down. Austin and Vicky were exhausted as they cleaned up what little food was left. They finish cleaning, rotated the time in the shower, and got comfortable in the bed. They were passed out before any bedroom playing could even come to mind.

Chapter 3.

"Ding! Ding! Ding!" The alarm sounds off. Austin opens his eyes while yarning, stretching, and sitting up in his bed. As he wiped his eyes he noticed Vicky was no longer beside him. He got up to walk to the bedroom and he could smell the aroma of fresh coffee so he walked into the kitchen instead. "Good morning baby. You're up early. I just knew I was going to have to drag you out the bed when we got up this morning." He said as he wrapped his arms around Vicky's body. "I bet. Especially since I didn't get any sleep until you stopped snoring like a bear." She said laughing while drying their coffee mugs. "Baby, I'm going to hop in the shower. Your coffee and breakfast is on the table." "Well, since we have plenty of time. How about you be my breakfast and coffee this morning?" "That would be great." She said leaning over giving Austin a soft kiss on the lips. "But, I have a meeting with the new hire and I have to get my project in order so she will understand everything." "Well, what if I be fast. It can be quick babe." He said, trying to convince Vicky. "Baby you're always fast and quick." She said, while smiling as she slowly escaped from Austin's arms. She then eased out of the kitchen and went into the bathroom. "Oh, you have jokes this morning?" Austin asked, as he set down at the kitchen table. Trying to come up with a way to seduce his wife, he thought, "Damn, I can't get no play around here, Fuck it. I'm just going to walk in and take a shower with Vicky." He got up from the kitchen table and made his way to the bedroom. He began taking off his boxers as he opened the door and noticed the bedroom was steamed up and smelled just

43

like Vicky's lavender and honey shampoo. Austin started walking closer to the shower curtain. He stops and peeped in the shower to look at Vicky. She was rubbing and washing her body. Checking out Vicky's beautiful body, eyeing her curves and long wet hair, he starts to stiffen up. He slowly made his way in the shower while Vicky washed her face. She turned around wiping her face, freeing it from soap and shampoo before she opened her eyes. "Ah!" Vicky yelled! "Austin! You scared me! Why are you in the shower? Why are you creeping up on me like some pervert?" Shocked at Vicky's reaction, Austin said, "Well I thought I'd come and get our day started off good with some morning loving." Vicky looked at Austin while the water was still running down her body. "Austin, I told you I was busy and I was trying to get to work early. And other thing. You didn't even brush your teeth. Now the bathroom smell like breath and steam." She pulled back the curtain and stepped out the shower. "I'm sure the soap will help out with your morning loving." She said, walking out of the bathroom. In the bedroom, she had her pants suit hanging up already pressed for the day. Vicky set on the foot of the bed, oiling her body with coconut oil. She put her skin tight black thong on along with the matching black bra. Laying back on the bed she placed her soft and smooth legs into her black thigh high stockings that complimented her thong and bra. She headed to the closet to put on her pants suit when Austin walked in and said, "Damn baby. I thought you were mad. But now that I see what you have on, I might have a second chance." Vicky looked back and said, "No, baby I'm not mad. And no, baby you don't have a second chance this morning. I just have an important day today." Austin looked and asked, "So that outfit is not for me?" Vicky stopped, sighed, and turned around saying, "No baby, this is definitely not an outfit. It's just some old underwear and bra." Austin sat on the bed and said, "Shitting me. That looks like you just took the tags off." Vicky smiled and said, "Baby, they look new because I still have the juice. The person makes the clothes. The clothes don't make the person." They both laughed as Austin replied, "Well you must be a hell of a person because you making the old rags look like new tags." He hopped off the bed and made his way to Vicky, wrapping his arms around her once more. Vicky said, "Austin, stop being thirsty. I told you I'm busy and rushing." "Calm down." He said while he still held Vicky in his arms. He started to whisper in Vicky ear, "Baby, I just want to let you know that I think you are the most beautiful woman in the world. I want to say that I'm sorry for my actions, knowing that this is a busy day for you. I just want you to know that I love you and respect you as a person. I respect your work and I apologize for being an ass this morning." Austin kissed Vicky on her cheek softly. He then released her from his arms and said, "I'll go to the kitchen and fix you some fresh coffee for your drive to work." Vicky smiled and said "Thank you." as she pulled her suit down from off of the door. When Austin came into the kitchen, Vicky's phone vibrated. It was a text that read "Lunch? You want to try a new spot?" The number did not appear with a name but Austin knew that Vicky had plenty of clients so he did not think anything of it. He continued to make Vicky's cup of coffee and turned to make his way back to the bedroom. Before he could leave the kitchen, Vicky

45

walked in fully dressed. "Austin? Have you seen my phone?" She asked nervously. "Umm, yeah Vicky, it's by the coffee maker. You had some text about lunch." He told Vicky. Vicky stopped in her tracks. "What!?" Vicky asked with worry on her face. "Did you read it? Who was it from? Where did they say lunch was at?" She asked as she rushed to the coffee maker. Austin shrugged his shoulders and said. "I don't know. Something about a new spot or something. Why? What's wrong? I figured it was a client or something. I was coming to the bedroom to let you know." Grabbing the phone with a feeling of relief. Vicky replied, "Nothing is wrong baby. It's a client that I've been waiting on. That's all." Looking at Vicky, Austin said, "Must be an important client. I hope you getting something good out the deal." She smirked and said, "I get good things out of all my deals baby. You know I grind for mine." She walked over to give Austin a hug and a juicy kiss on the lips. Austin started laughing. "What's so funny?" "I still haven't brush my teeth." "You are just trifling." Vicky said laughing and walking out of the kitchen. "I'm going to work, Love you!" "Love you too." Austin said as he walked to the bedroom. Vicky made her way to work an hour early. She beat traffic and had more time to organize what the guidelines were for the new hire. An hour or so passed and Vicky heard a knocked on her office door. "Come in." She yelled. "Hi. Are you Victoria Roberts?" "Yes. Yes, I am and who might you be?" "My name is Cynthia. Cynthia Heights. I'm the new hire from Miami." Cynthia explain. "Oh yes, how are you? You are very beautiful. I wasn't expecting a woman with such beauty to want to up and leave Miami like that. Honestly, I was expecting someone who looked fair and ran out of options in Miami." Vicky said with a laugh. "I mean, when they told me you were coming from Miami and was willing to move in such a short notice. I was like, wow. Should I be worried?" Cynthia laughed with Vicky as she held a fake smile, judging Vicky on her wonderful first impression. "Well Vicky, sometimes you have to get out of the box and seek things to see what's exactly right for you." "Oh touché. Well Cynthia, you are going to be my right hand woman from now on. I have plans for you and I. Especially in this market, with our clients being mostly men. They are going to see you and fall right in your hands. They're all dogs that want to be wolves. But like all animals, they all need females and we are the bitches that they want. So are you ready to make this money and enjoy our take over in this market?" Cynthia looked at Vicky as she felt rude to judge her so fast. She responded, "Money is my first name." She smiled and stuck her hand out for Vicky to shake hands. Vicky accepted Cynthia's kind gesture. "Welcome to my world." "Thank you, Victoria". Cynthia said. "Please, call me Vicky. So, this is the plan for the day. I'm going to show you around the office. Then we have a meeting with Richard Gas & Oil Company. We are going to team up and let them hang themselves. I'm sure you received the email about their company. You and I are going to convince them that we need 15% more from them, which will give me and you a sale bonus on my next check and your first check." Cynthia smiled and said, "That sounds great! But how will we guarantee that we will get the 15%? I read my report on Richard Gas & Oil. Their stock is down almost 30% and that doesn't include their pipe that just snapped. That alone is going to cost them a

47

fortune." Vicky smirked and said, "You told me all that to tell me what? Cynthia, please realize that your report and what you're talking about is a company. A company that is still up and running. We get them to up us 15% now. Give them $250k for a hand out to help them and include a little interest. In six to eight months, we mark another 15% and they still owe us $250k plus interest from the hand out. The big guys see you made them 30% in Richard Gas & Oil Company less than one year on the job. Trust me. Someone is going to be buying you a Porsche truck." Cynthia looked at Vicky, impressed with her knowledge. She saw her drive and how she planned a perfect sneak attack for 30% of someone's company. "I'm overly intrigued. Back home, no one would have thought to pull such a move on a company like that. Let alone on Richard Gas & Oil. Especially when they're wounded." Vicky smiled. "Thank you, but this move isn't just for me. It's for you also." "How so?" Cynthia asked. "These people need to know that we are not to be played with. They need to know that we will help them in a friendly manner but don't try to take advantage of us. Most importantly, they need to know that even though you are new with our company. You won't take any shit. Sharks come out the womb swimming and today you are going to show them that you are a damn shark. Besides, when I'm on vacation. I don't need a wounded animal running my jungle. Now, let me give you a short tour on the way to your office." "Great." Cynthia said, as the both walked out of Vicky's office. They walked down the hall into an open area where the cubicles were. As the passed the cubicles, Cynthia said, "Well, I'm right at home. This is nicer then the Miami cubicles. Where is mine?" Vicky stopped and looked back at Cynthia. "Do you know what position you applied for?" Cynthia chuckled and said, "Well yes, AMS. Assistant Marketing Specialist." Vicky looked at Cynthia. "I'm the market specialist for this entire company. Our teams must run numbers by me before they try and market our business out of the country. Do you not see what floor we are on? You are my assistant, but not my assistant that gets coffee. You are the assistant that helps me market this entire company. Your resume was perfect. Why would you think less of your position?" In shock, Cynthia stood there and said. "I was assistant in Miami under my director. But it was just assisting my section of the building. I didn't know I was going to be on top so soon, that's all." "Are you going to be able to handle such a position?" Vicky asked. Cynthia looked Vicky in her eyes. She knew that if she said the wrong thing, Vicky would send her home without giving her the time of day. So Cynthia spoke with confidence. "Vicky, I can handle this position with my hands tied behind my back. You've seen my resume and you know why you picked me. I handled the interview quite well. My section of the building went up sixty-five percent in market sales, all because of my ideas and hard work. You're putting me in a position to do everything I did in Miami but with bigger stakes and more opportunities. I've controlled a unit that wasn't shit before I got there and now they're on top and I still haven't gotten acknowledged for my work. So with all due respect, I can handle this damn position with no problem." Vicky looked at Cynthia and smirked. "Well, let me show you to your office." They left the open area and walked to another hallway. "Why are our offices so far apart?" Cynthia asked. "Well, corners of the building aren't close together you know." Vicky said as she smiled. Playing it cool and keeping calm, Cynthia couldn't believe that she was going from a crappy cubicle to a fifty seventh floor corner office. God is good she thought to herself. They finally arrived at the corner office and it was a sight to see. The office was extremely large and faced the south of the city. There was a large glass desk. The cabinets were steal and black. They matched the chairs to a T. You could see the traffic on the bridge crossing the famous James River. "This is amazing. Is this my office?" Cynthia asked. "The south side always looks nice with the view of the river. I figured, since it will get a little stressful from time to time being a new hire, you may need the view to relax or to unwind. If you know what I mean." Cynthia looked at Vicky and said. "I don't follow." Vicky folded her arms and raised her eyebrows. "You have a lot to learn here with me. The business is just the first part. Tell me. What is the first thing you thought about your desk?" Vicky asked. Cynthia struggled her shoulders. Then said. "It's very pretty, big, and looks sturdy." Vicky said "Exactly. I couldn't have said it better myself. Just like a bed without the cushion of course." "Oh, oh ok. I see now. I follow you. Well Vicky, I don't have a man right now." "So, you've never been married?" Vicky asked. Unfolding her arms as she waited for an answer. "That's a subject I like to stay away from." Cynthia nervously chuckled. "But to answer your question, yes I was married at one point in my life. But that's neither here nor there. I moved forward with life. Even through it's an adventures." "I can understand that. Once a woman has made her mind up, it's to the races." Vicky replied.

"Yeah." Cynthia agreed as she dazed off looking at the city's view. "Well feel free to unwind when you feel the need to. Just try not to do it on days when we have major meetings. Another thing. Sometimes you don't need a man to relieve your stress." Vicky said as she winked her eye. Cynthia smiled. "Yeah, my college days are over!" "Well, you do learn a lot in college that helps you with your future. But that's neither here nor there. Look, I know this is all new so take a few minutes to soak in your new office." Vicky encourage. "I will." Cynthia said, feeling a little weird about the small pass Vicky had just made. After about 20 minutes of peace, Cynthia heard a knock at her office door. "Come in!" Cynthia yelled. A man walked in. "Hi. Ms. Heights. My name is Travis Jenkins. I am your assistant. If you need anything let me know." Travis was a very handsome man. He was dark skinned with a low cut. Cynthia could tell that he was very fit by the way his tailored suit hugged his muscles. She thought to herself, "Mr. Travis Jenkins, you can be my stress reliever when I'm in need." Glimpsing down at his pants, she was curious about his penis size. She then looked back up to Travis' face. Cynthia smiled and said. "Nice belt. Travis, you can call me Cynthia. We all are grown here. No need to put Mr. or Ms. on things." Travis smiled and said. "Ms. Heights. I mean Cynthia, I understand. It's just a respect thing. And if you need anything, please let me know. I am here to help you help Mrs. Roberts." "Yes, I understand." Cynthia replied as Travis exited the office. Some time had passed since Cynthia's refreshing encounter with Travis when Vicky knocked on the door and made her way into Cynthia's office. "Cynthia, let's look around before our meeting starts. I have some people I would like you to meet." "Sure." Cynthia replied as she made her way to Vicky. Vicky began to escort her around the company's fifty-fourth floor. Vicky went from desk to desk politely introducing the staff to Cynthia. After the tour of the floor, Vicky and Cynthia went over the game plan for their meeting with Richard Gas & Oil Company. Shortly after, Vicky and Cynthia exchanged points, the meeting with Richard Gas & Oil Company was held and it went exactly how Vicky said it would. The women walked out of the meeting with their heads held high. They proved why they were so successful in what they did with selling, trading, and buying market value. "Let's go to my office." Vicky said, as Cynthia followed her. Upon entering Vicky's office, she told Cynthia to shut the door and grab to champagne glasses. In shock, Cynthia said, "We are going to drink at work?" "We are not getting drunk. Just a little champagne for celebration. Wait, you never drink to celebrate at work?" "No, not even a little. Then again, we did drink sparkling grape juice." Cynthia replied as Vicky burst out laughing. "I celebrate birthdays with champagne for my employees that work in my section. Respect and love, I share with all." Vicky said while pouring champagne and handing Cynthia a glass. "To a new start and looking outside the box." Vicky toasted. Accepting the toasted, Cynthia raised her glass with a smile and said, "To a new start and looking outside the box." Right when their glasses hit together, Vicky's phone started vibrating on the table. "Oh, what time is it?" Vicky asked. "Oh, it's a little after one p.m." Cynthia responded. Vicky rushed over to her phone. Checking the text, she looked up at Cynthia and asked. "We plan to be partners in crime, right?" "Umm, yeah. Why?" Vicky hit the intercom on her desk. "Yes Mrs. Roberts?" The front desk asked. "Brittney, call for my car to come around. Ms. Heights and I are coming down for lunch." "Yes, I will get right on it and congrats on the Richard deal." Brittney said as she ended the call. "What's so criminal about a lunch?" Cynthia asked. "I'll let you figure it out." Vicky said as they headed downstairs to the car. They drove across town to the Croaker Spot. Once they arrived, Cynthia could see there was a line. She figured there was going to be a small wait until they walked to the attendant and Vicky said, "Hi. I am Mrs. Smith. I'm here with the Smiths and their plus one." The waitress said "Yes, follow me." "Mrs. Smith?" Cynthia thought to herself. "Vicky, that's not your name. Who is Mrs. Smith?" Vicky smiled and said. "I'll let you figure this thing out on your own. You might need a Mr. Smith one day." Confused, Cynthia started to think, "maybe it's her husband and they have a kinky relationship to keep things exciting." As they arrived at the table, Vicky said, "Hey baby. How are you?" Mr. Smith smiled and said, "I'm doing well Mrs. Smith." Mr. Smith stood up and pulled out Vicky's chair. He asked, "And who might this beautiful lady be?" Sticking her hand out, Cynthia said. "Hello. Please to meet you. I am Cynthia. And you are?" The man smiled and said, "I am, Mr. Smith." Cynthia sat down as she was unsure if Vicky was having an affair or not. None the less, Cynthia went along with it and said, "Well, nice to meet you Mr. Smith. How is the food here?" "It's great. The food, drinks and service is wonderful here." Vicky answered. "Not as wonderful as you." Mr. Smith said giving Vicky a soft kiss on the check. When Mr. Smith kissed Vicky, Cynthia knew right away that Mr. Smith was Vicky's husband. Happy for their relationship, Cynthia said. "You guys look great together." "Too bad it's only under the table." Mr. Smith said as he and Vicky laughed. Cynthia looked at Mr. Smith and wanted to ask "what do you mean," but before she could, the waitress came to the table. "Hello everyone. How are you all? What would you be starting off with today?" They all went searching thru the menus. The waitress took everyone's order one by one. As the waitress was leaving, Vicky's phone vibrated. She looked down to see who it was. Mr. Smith took a glance as well and they both looked shocked. Cynthia asked, "Are you guys ok?" "Yes, yes." Mr. Smith said, as he got up from the table telling the ladies he was going to the restroom. Cynthia smiled and said, "Ok." As Mr. Smith exited the table. "So, what's up?" Cynthia asked. "Nothing, nothing at all." Vicky said, grabbing the waitress as she was walking by. "Excuse me. Can I get another glass of white wine?" "Sure thing." Then waitress said. "Are you sure you're ok? You and Mr. Smith looked a little disturbed when you got that call." "Girl, its nothing. Family issues." "Oh, I can definitely understand that. My family is crazy as hell back in Miami." Cynthia said as they both laughed. Mr. Smith walked up and asked, "What's so funny?" Vicky said, "Cynthia was just telling me about her family in Miami and how all families have their issues." "Oh yeah? How so?" Mr. Smith asked. "You know, just crazy stuff. The normal family drama." "Yeah, I get that." Mr. Smith said as the food arrived. "Looking good." Vicky said. Cynthia agreed and said, "You guys brought me here trying to mess my figure up." They all laughed. Mr. Smith said, "No, it's going to take a lot to mess that figure up." When he said that, Cynthia looked at Vicky, surprised she let her husband say that. Then Vicky added, "That is a nice figure." Mr. Smith. "Yeah, because you could be overweight, like the lady sitting behind me." They all looked and laughed. Cynthia said, "We all are going to go hell for laughing at her." Still laughing, Mr. Smith said, "Yeah, but she going to get there first because she's going to fall faster." Vicky chuckled as she sipped her wine, causing herself to choke. Cynthia said, "See God is starting with you." They all laughed once more before they began to eat, drank and share more laughs. They finished eating and walked out of the restaurant. Cynthia was expecting the married couple to kiss and say their good-byes, but they did not. Mr. Smith walked off and said, "Good-bye." then disappeared in the afternoon sun light. "Man, ole man, he's fine." Cynthia said while laughing with Vicky. "You should see him naked." Vicky said. Cynthia laugh and said, "No, I'm not one to steps on anybody's toes. That is your husband. I saw the rings. He is fine but I'll leave him up to you." "Well, ok." Vicky said, still smiling as they walked to her car. "Where did you go shopping for your husband, I need the website?" Cynthia jokingly asked, as they hopped in the car. Vicky smiled and said, "I shop at a different site for him. My husband's site is a different google search." "Wait." Cynthia said. "That was not your husband?" "No, and you are the only one who knows that. The last person who was in your position was Jimmy Sanders. And if he knew I was having an affair, he would have tried to blackmail me to get in my pants or take my job the first chance he got. Some men are just awful." "Umm yeah, I know." Cynthia agreed as she thought to herself. Some women are too. They pulled off and headed back to the office. "So, what happened to you and your husband? You never told me." Vicky asked. Cynthia looked at Vicky and said, "Umm, we just wanted different things you know. I wanted a family and he wanted a sports car kind of thing. We ended in an 'ok' way I guess. Wish I could have change some things though. I'm sure we would have stayed married for a long time if I didn't go and do what I did." "What did you do?" Vicky asked. Cynthia froze up as if she did not mean to say that. Before she could get any answer out, Vicky's phone rang, interrupting their conversation. "Oh, this is my husband. The real one. Give me a second." Vicky said. "Hello. Hey baby, I was just thinking about you." Vicky said. She carried on a conversation as Cynthia sat in the passenger, thinking to herself, "I can't believe Vicky is cheating all in the open. I can't believe she is cheating at all. Her husband is probably a good man. Damn, another good man taken off the market due to some reckless chick who could give no fucks." Vicky got off of the phone. She asked, "What were we talking about? Cynthia knew she didn't want to tell Vicky anything more about her personal life. So she quickly changed the subject. "I'm not sure. But anyway, I've been meaning to tell you that I love your shoes." Excited about the shoes, Vicky rambled on about how nice they feel on the inside and how comfortable they were. They finally arrived back at the office. The ladies got out of the car and went into the building to finish up their day. "That was a great lunch Vicky." Cynthia said. "Yeah, no problem. I like you Cynthia. I don't know what it is, but I do. I'm glad you enjoyed the lunch. Now go and take a load off. Go get your new office together. I'm going to go over some things in my office. I'll see you before I leave to go home." Vicky explained. "Thanks, I really appreciate that Vicky." The two ladies headed to their offices. Cynthia made her way to her office and ran into Brad at her office door. "Hey, my name is Brad. I manage operations here. You're the new hire that's in charge, right?" "Well, yes and no." Cynthia said. Brad smiled and said, "That's a great answer, I guess. But what answer is what?" Cynthia said. "I'm not in charge, but I am a new hire." Laughing, he said, "Don't take me so literal. I know who you are. Well, I'll let you get settled in. Maybe we could grab lunch sometime." Cynthia laugh and asked, "So, you came over here with a game plan huh?" "I wouldn't say game plan but I was expecting to ask you to lunch." Brad said. "Yeah, maybe. But I do have somethings to do. So, I'm going to go take care of that." "Yeah, sure thing. I'm going to have to hold you to that 'maybe.'" Brad said while walking away smiling. Cynthia smiled and said, "Yeah ok." As she headed inside her new office. After sorting and moving things around, it was four-thirty P.M and it was time to get off. "Oh, what a first day" Cynthia thought as she walked out of the building getting into her car. Cynthia figured she would check out a happy hour. She was not going to do much when she got home but unpack and sleep, so she went riding in the area called "The Fan in Richmond." Cynthia overheard some people talking about going to "The Fan" for happy hour. She finally stopped at a local bar after riding around for a short while. She sat at the bar and ordered herself a drink. Cynthia heard a man's voice. "Well, well, well... Look who it is." Cynthia looked over her shoulder only to see

Thomas. Rolling her eyes, she said. "What do you want? Out of all the bars in Richmond, you had to come to this one right here." "Well, I'm happy to see you too." He said smiling as he sat at the bar beside Cynthia. Before she could speak again, Thomas said "Look Cynthia..." "Oh, you remember my name?" Cynthia asked cutting Thomas off. "Yeah, I do. I'm not here to start anything. I just came to the bar to get a drink while I think about some things. How about this for starters, I'm sorry for how I acted at Lowe's the other day. I was wrong and I apologize." Cynthia looked at Thomas and said, "Well, that's a start. Everyone deserve a second chance at something." Relieved, Thomas said. "Thanks for accepting my apology. Your next drink is on me." Cynthia said, "Oh no. That's fine. I'm leaving after this drink." Looking stressed, Thomas asked "Well, can you talk to me and give me an opinion on something before you leave? I rather hear the truth from someone I don't know. Like someone who's looking in from the outside. It wouldn't be like you're showing any favoritism, you know?" "I guess we can talk for a quick second, what's bothering you?" Cynthia asked. Thomas got the bartender's attention and ordered a drink. He then looked back at Cynthia and said, "Have you ever been scared that you would be alone for the rest of your life?" Cynthia looked at Thomas and said, "I think that now." Shocked, Thomas asked "Really? How? I'm sure there are plenty of guys that is willing to take you out to wine and dine you." She answered, "And then after, they want to have sex with me. Then make me some one that they can call to have sex with when they feel the urge. So then I began to feel like the man is not going to love me for me, rather than my beauty and my

58

body." "I can understand that." Thomas said, grabbing his drink as bartender placed it on the bar. "I think I'm going to be alone because I'm in love with someone I shouldn't be." Thomas said, looking at Cynthia. "Why? Why do think that you shouldn't be loving this person? Are they married Thomas?" Cynthia asked as she frowned. "No, no. I don't do married women. I don't want that karma." Picking up her drink, Cynthia said, "Yeah, trust me. It's a bitch. Hey, are you going to give me that drink or what?" Laughing, Thomas said. "I thought you wasn't staying long?" Cynthia answered and said, "That was before when I thought you were an asshole. You are just starting to change that." "Well, I guess it's a good thing that I got a second chance then. It was only right for me to try and make things right between us." They both laugh as Cynthia said, "Yeah, I guess you're right." "So, tell me about this woman? How long you guys been dating?" Thomas said, "Well, we've been dating for about 2 years but we've just been taking our time." "So why you think you shouldn't be loving her?" Cynthia asked. "Because I know it would mess up a lot of things relationship wise." Thomas explain. "So, she is married?" "No, Cynthia. What's up with you and married people cheating?" Thomas asked as he laughed. "I just was with someone who was playing their husband like a tennis game. Whatever he threw at her, she had the perfect hit to come back with." "Damn." Thomas said, shaking his head. "I would hate to be him." "Yeah, tell me about it. She replied. "Well look, I think if you guys are good friends and she loves you, maybe you guys should be together. It doesn't make sense toying around and playing with each other." She said. "Cynthia, you're right. I think I'm going

59

to say something when I get the balls to." "All that talk you had when you were being Mr. Rude, now you're telling me you don't have the balls to tell a woman that you want to make it right and be together." Thomas chuckled and said. "Only if it was that easy. How about we relax and sip these drinks and let them take our minds off this stuff? It's starting to be a little too much for me." Cynthia agreed. An hour or so went by as they talked, laughed and had a few more drinks. Cynthia looked at the time. "Well, it's getting a little late Thomas." Thomas agreed. "Yeah, I guess you're right." "You're not that bad." Cynthia said. "Maybe you would have had a shot if you was this guy from the start. But you were an asshole." They both laughed and Thomas said, "Yeah, you're right. I should have been more, cool." Thomas grabbed a pen and wrote his name and number on a napkin. "Give me a call whenever you want to talk or just hang out." Cynthia took the napkin and said, "Maybe I will, but I'm not making any promises." She got up from the bar stool. Thomas chuckled and said, "Cynthia this was a great first date." Laughing, Cynthia said, "And there's the Thomas I know. You just had to go and mess up the evening" "Good bye, Mr. Rude." "Good bye Mrs. Right." Thomas said, as the both chuckled and smiled. Cynthia headed out of the bar and made her way home to unpack, leaving Thomas at the bar to soak in his thoughts.

Chapter 4.

"Ring, ring, ring!" Austin's phone went off as he struggled to find it. He grabbed the phone from under an old shirt, picking it up as he wiped the cold out of his eye. He hears Thomas. "Hello? Hellooo?" "Yeah man, what's up? Damn. Do you know what time it is?" Austin asked. "Yeah, I know it's like six something, almost seven. Damn, you're normally up." Sitting up on the edge of the bed, Austin asked, "T, what's so important that you had to call me this early?" Excited, Thomas said, "Yo, you not going to believe who I ran into at the bar yesterday evening." Frustrated after hearing what Thomas was calling so early for, Austin said, "So you called me this early in the morning to tell me about some old chick that you use to smash. T, this shit could have waited until later." "Nah, nah, this couldn't." Thomas said, still sounding filled with excitement. "Man, so who is the chick and why is she so important?" Austin said while standing up to walk into the bathroom. "Umm, I would say she's important because she curved me the first time and now I have a second chance to get them cheeks." "Ayo T, it's early as fuck. I don't have time for your context clues. Who is this chick?" Austin asked as he yawned while using the bathroom. "Ok, ok. Remember the Lowe's chick?" "Who? The Lowe's chick?" with curiosity in his voice. After a quick second, Austin said "oh, you talking about Brook, with the nice ass? The one that was the manager there? Word, I know you hype. That bitch bad but she still not worth my morning call." Austin laughed. "No fool, Cynthia. Your love bird. Miss golden girl." Austin's face went from laughter to serious as he remembered the beauty of Cynthia. Playing it off without showing any emotions, Austin said "Damn T. It's your move on the board. How are you going to act?" Hype about the whole thing Thomas said, "Nigga! I'm going to act accordingly. See, what I did was that nice and gentle shit you were talking about. To be honest, that shit work like a charm. I presented myself as a nice guy, but still had the dog in me." Thomas said while laughing. "Yeah, how so?" Austin asked. "Well Mr. Austin, I slightly opened up to her and she loved it. We stayed at the bar and kicked it for a few hours. I mean, talking about a lot of things I thought was bullshit but she thought it was real." "So you played her?" Austin asked. "Ok ok, I'm not going to lie. I spoke the truth about some things, but yeah I played her. Then I kicked my number to her before she left. I doubt she call this week but I know for sure she's going to call next week. Then its game time after that nigga!" "Congrats, but just to let you know, you're going about this the wrong way." Thomas sighed. "What do you mean Austin? Here you go with this hating shit. What am I doing that's so wrong?" "You do know how old you are? You need to be trying to make her your wife. She is super bad, got shit going for herself and knows what she wants out of life. Unlike them young hoes that you play mind games with. Let's be serious, she's a 'hold you down if you keep it real' type of woman. You know you got that vibe. That's all I'm saying. But hey, I wish you the best of luck with this one my friend. You must remember she is a grown woman and not a fresh out of college dreamer. And one more thing, what would you have spoken the truth about in a conversation with her anyway? She is all about emotions and feelings. I know you didn't tell her you love someone." Austin laughed while waiting for an answer. "Nigga, I do love someone. It's just difficult." said Thomas, sounding snappy. "Whoa, Calm down. Now if you supposed to be in love, who is she then T? Tell me who she is and I promise I'll leave you alone about this whole thing." "It's somebody." Thomas said under his breathe. "Say what?" Austin asked. Before Thomas could answer he had shut the conversation down. "Yo, one of my clients calling. I have to go." Knowing what Thomas was doing, Austin agreed. "Get that money T, I'll talk to you later." Austin proceeded to wash his face and brush his teeth. After, he headed back into the bedroom to hop on his wife. When he got in the room, he noticed that Vicky was not there. He saw a small hand written note on his night stand that read: "Early day at the office, didn't want to wake you. Love you, talk to you soon." The note held a scent of perfume that he had brought Vicky earlier that summer. As the scent lingered in his nose, Austin began looking for a suit to put on for work. While in the closet, he grabbed for a belt that fell to the floor. Searching for the belt, Austin started moving around shoe boxes and a few of Vicky's heels. He finally found the belt and noticed a "Victoria's Secret" bag. Curious, Austin thought to himself, "this must be something new." while opening the bag. Austin dug deep, pulling out a black body suit with pink lip stick smeared on it. He ran through his thoughts, trying to remember when Vicky had put it on for him. It finally hit him. "Last Tuesday night." he thought to himself with a smile. He felt good as a man to have a beautiful wife that always dressed nice and kept the romance up. Austin got up and got dressed.

Before he headed to work, he made sure he contacted the nearest florist and ordered Vicky some "just because" flowers. A few hours passed and Austin was settled in at work. He noticed that he hadn't gotten a call, text or any sign of thank you from Vicky. So Austin called the florist to check if the flowers delivered. The florist confirmed that the flowers were delivered and someone signed for them. Austin was excited but also curious. He called Vicky's cell and there was no answer. More curious and less excited, he called Vicky's office. Cynthia picked up. "Hello, this is Ms. Heights. AMS manager, how can I help you?" "Oh hey," Austin said. "I think I called the wrong desk." "Well, who were you trying to reach?" "I'm trying to reach my wife, Victoria Roberts." Shocked, knowing that Vicky was out of the office doing god knows what, Cynthia knew she couldn't be a part of the reason Vicky got caught in her lies. She decided to cover for Vicky and told some of the truth. "Well yes, Mr. Roberts. I'm the new hire. When your wife is out of the office all calls are transferred to my desk. I am the person under Mrs. Roberts." "Oh ok, that makes sense." Austin said. "Well, Ms. Heights, do you happen to know where she is? I tried her cell but she didn't pick up." Covering for Vicky, Cynthia said, "Oh she's been in a board meeting on the other side of town for most of the morning. More than likely, she might still be there." "Oh ok, that must be the reason she left early today." Feeling awful, Cynthia agreed. Then changed the conversation and asked, "Would you like to leave a message?" "Umm. No, no thank you. I'll just wait to hear from her myself." "Sure thing Mr. Roberts" Cynthia replied. "Well, Ms. Height, I did send her flowers. Did they arrive?" Cynthia smiled and said, "I kind of figured you were calling about the flowers." Austin smiled on the other side of the phone. "Yeah, but please don't tell her I called about them." as he laughed a little. "They are beautiful. I signed for them and sat them right on her desk. No worries, your secret is safe with me Mr. Roberts." Cynthia said, as she felt bad for the man. "Thanks, I really appreciate it." "Hey, by the way. What's your name?" "Oh, how rude of me" Cynthia said. "Heights, is my last name." Before Cynthia could tell him her first name, Austin's line beeped. "Oh, I have to go. This is my wife on the other end Ms. Heights. It's was nice talking to you." "Yes, Mr. Roberts, it was" Cynthia said, as she was relieved to get off of the phone. Austin clicked over. "Hey baby. How are you?" I'm great baby, feeling wonderful. But I've been busy at the office all morning." Vicky said. "All morning?" Austin asked. "Yeah baby, why?" Oh, I just got off the phone with your new hire. She said you had a meeting across town or something." "Yeah, we had a meeting across town. But I'm on the tenth floor helping, Kyran Paste, on a new outlook at the company." A well performed lie that Vicky told Austin as she was getting off the elevator walking straight to Cynthia's office. "Oh ok, I'll see you when you get home," he said trying not to ruin the surprise for Vicky. "Ok, see you later baby." Vicky said as she walked right into Cynthia's office. "Hey." Vicky said. Cynthia immediately started, "I'm sorry! I couldn't think of anything but to say you were in a meeting." Vicky looked at Cynthia with a blank face, then started smiling. "Girl chill. I'm happy you said that because I was caught." said Vicky while laughing. Cynthia started smiling as she felt bad once more and thought to herself. "What have I started?" Hoping that she would not have to be a part of an affair anymore. She was torn so she decided to just nod, smile, and agree. Changing the conversation, Cynthia said, "Well let's go to your office. I believe it's a surprise there for you." Excited, Vicky asked, "Are you serious? Let's go!" The ladies left out of Cynthia's office and headed to Vicky's. They could see a bundle of red roses and Vicky started to get excited. "They are so beautiful." Vicky said. As they got closer, Vicky started smiling more. They entered her office and Vicky smiled as she looked at the bright red long stemmed roses, which were clipped fantastically well. The roses seemed to be measured perfectly, as they set in a silver vase that was decorated with mirror hearts. Vicky picked up the note and it read "just because." Excited, Vicky said, "I was just talking to Mr. Smith about some flowers and he got them. I can't believe it. I literally just said to him, 'some just because flowers would be great.' I need to call him right now." "These aren't from Mr. Smith, they are from your husband Mr. Roberts. He called to see if you had received them." Cynthia explained. Vicky's face suddenly looked disappointed. She sat down in her chair and said "Oh." Cynthia asked, "Don't you still think this is wonderful? I mean, you didn't even have to mention it to your husband. He just did it." "Well, I guess you're right." said Vicky, as she set a reminder to call Austin and thank him for the flowers. "I'll give him a call later. Let's get to business." Cynthia had caught on to the fact that Vicky wanting to call Mr. Smith now, but Mr. Roberts later. She thought to herself, "what a great man gone to waste." Then went along with Vicky as she started talking about a new company project that was worth millions. They went over contracts, numbers, and a vision of what they could present in the new big project. Cynthia really did like working with Vicky, but she knew her mischievous ways would catch up to her. After hours passed, it was time for the team to go home. Vicky eventually called Austin as she got in her car. She thanked him, yet still not as excited. Cynthia left out right behind Vicky as the office closed. Still not believing how she was an asset to a cheating wife. Cynthia figure she would go to another bar. Somewhere not so popular. She did not want another run in with Thomas. Not that she didn't enjoy the conversation, she just wanted some time to have a drink and get a cool bar vibe without getting hit on. She drove through the streets of Richmond looking for a hole in the wall bar with a good top shelf drink. She noticed a handsome man right before he walked into a bar that did not have a name on it. Cynthia thought to herself, "this must be a sign." She circled the block until she found a good parking spot and headed to the bar. Walking up to the bar, Cynthia started thinking, "maybe this is not a good idea." But as she got closer she could smell the food the aroma attracted her. She stood looking at the outside of the bar amazed at how it really looked like a hole in the wall. Cynthia walked in and noticed that it was very nice in the inside. The pool table, bar stools and even the wood floors looked almost brand new. The televisions were nice and big. The low lights set an amazing look as if they were in an old mob movie. The place seems like it was meant to be frowned on from the outside so you would be amazed when you walked inside. Cynthia noticed that it was not a crowded place and she loved it. As she walked over to the bar and spoke to those she passed, she realized she didn't see the attractive man. Thinking little of it, Cynthia sat at the bar. A rough bearded man was the bartender. He came over and said, "Well, hello ma'am. I take it you're a new comer. Welcome to my place Joe's Whole." Cynthia started laughing. "That's the name of this place? Joe's Whole?" "Yeah, why?" the bartender asked. "Oh nothing, that's a great name. Now I get it. It looks bad on the outside for a reason." The bartender looked at Cynthia and asked, "What? What are you trying to say? My place looks bad? I worked hard for this building and busted my ass every day to keep it up and running." Cynthia went into shocked as the man started to get mad. Cynthia explained, "No, the place is nice. I'm sorry. I'm so sorry sir." The man started laughing and said "Sweet heart, I'm just pulling your chain. I'm a retired business man with nothing to do but spend money. Hell, if I don't do it before I die, my wife will." Cynthia was relived as she began laughing with Joe. Still laughing, the bartender seen a man walking from the bathroom area and said, "There's my partner in crime." Still holding a light smile from joking with Joe, Cynthia turned around. There he stood, right in front of her, Austin. "Well hello Miss Cynthia." Austin said, as he sat right next to her. "You have to be kidding me." "What?" Austin asked. "I just ran into your reckless friend yesterday and now I'm running into you here. What are the odds?" Cynthia asked. Austin nodded at Cynthia. "Yeah, he told me you guys talked. You're becoming popular around Richmond, huh?" "I guess." Cynthia replied. "Well anyway, enough of being so uptight. Have a drink and relax. Oh, and Cynthia? The odds of finding me here are very high. This is one of the only bars I go to in the city. Not many people know about this place and I like it like that." Joe hopped in the conversation. "Young lady, it's pretty nice to know the people that come in and out your bar. The college kids will get drunk and trash your place. So we never put a sign out. Well, it's on the door, but we keep the door open during the summer. You'll kind of have to already know about this place. Right partner?" Joe asked as he nodded towards Austin. "That's right Joe." Cynthia said "Hold on. Why does he keep calling you partner? Do you own this bar?" Cynthia asked. "No, not the whole thing, just half." "So does Thomas know about this?" "No, he doesn't. And I would love if you keep it that way." Joe cut in and said, "That damn Thomas would have all kinds of woman and parties going on if he knew about this. Look baby girl, if you can keep this between us and not Thomas, the first drink is on the house every time you come in." Cynthia looked around at the bar and looked back at the bartender. She felt a sense of comfort and quickly said, "You got it!" She reached her hand over the bar, shaking his hand as they sealed the deal. Cynthia turned and looked at Austin with her hand out. Austin looked at Cynthia with a straight face that turn into a smile and shook her hand. Then Joe said, "Let me grab us some shot glasses." "Oh no, no shots for me" Austin said. Joe then looked at Cynthia and told her, "Baby girl, can you tell Austin to stop being a pussy!" Cynthia laughed and looked at Austin and said, "Stop being a pussy." Austin laughed and told Joe that he would only have one shot. "Don't have me in here fucked up." One shot lead to two shots. The second lead to a third, then it keep going." Joe laughed walking leaving Cynthia and Austin alone. They started talking. "So how's your new job going?" Austin asked. "The job itself is great." "What do you mean by that?" Austin asked. "Well, I actually love working with my new team. It's just, I work more one on one with my boss. That gets me. And man, that bitch is the devil of relationships." Austin started laughing and asked, "What do you mean by that?" Cynthia replied, "Don't get me wrong, the chick knows her work, but she's cheating on her husband. When I say cheating...The women have times, places and events when she cheats. They even have code names. Mr. & Mrs Smith, like the movie." Austin started laughing. Cynthia continued, "The bad thing is, her husband is a great man." Austin said, "Well how do you know? Not so great if she'd cheating on him, huh?" Cynthia responded, "Ever sense I've been there, the man has been doing things for her. I mean, the whole nine yards. I just can tell that he is a great guy. I'm not sure if my boss is just fucking the side man, in a relationship, or having an affair. The sad part is that's he married too." "Damn, now that's a fucked up situation," Austin said. "Yeah, I know." Cynthia agreed. "So what's the company called?" Austin asked. "Oh no! I definitely won't be telling you that. Especially with me not being from around here. You might know one of them." Austin started laughing and agreed. "Yeah, well I guess you have good reason. So, why aren't you still married?" Austin asked. "That is the question I've been asked in almost every conversation lately. How about we not talk marriage." "Ok, let's talk beauty." "Beauty?" Cynthia asked. "Yeah, beauty." Austin said while smiling. "Why is it that all beautiful woman, like yourself, always come around when men are married?" Cynthia said, "Austin, was that a pick up line?" Austin laughed and answered, "No, I'm happily with my wife. But let's talk in general. Man or woman, boy or girl, a person could be single and never meet or see an attractive, fun person. As soon as they get into a relationship and can't lay a finger on anyone else, here comes that attractive, fun person." "Oh ok, I see," Cynthia said. "Well maybe it's in the stars to make a person love harder." Austin said, "Now that doesn't make sense." "But yes it does. Maybe that person you're with is not for you, but you love them. The new person of beauty is for you to cheat with and get caught, so you can love the next person harder." "How so?" Austin asked. While he looked at the time and noticed it was late. "Well, it's like this," Cynthia explained. "Everyone misses someone, wants someone or crave something when they leave or threaten to leave. It's like they realize that they were wrong for cheating. They will either hurt and move on or get forgiveness and love harder and do right because they learned the true value of how important their lover is. If they move on, the cycle will continue until they run across the right person." Looking at Cynthia, Austin said, "Damn, I never even looked at it that way. I mean, but I've never even experienced the cycle." "Funny things can happen anywhere and at any time," Cynthia finished explaining. "Is that right?" Austin asked, as they made eye contact. Cynthia then turned her bar stool towards Austin and asked, "What if I'm your cycle?" While placing her hands on his as they both starred in a dazed. Austin responded, "Playing a dangerous spin is usually accompanied with playing a dangerous cycle." The tension grew between the two as Cynthia leaned over inches from Austin's face. "All things can be tamed. You just have to know what you

71

are taming. In this case, a cycle of passion. You think you can control it before it breaks?" Cynthia was so close that she could pucker her lips and kiss Austin. Before Austin could answer Cynthia, Joe the bartender interrupted. "Austin it's nine." Austin answered, "Nine? Yeah, I have to go. Joe, put her on my tab." Austin got up from the bar, grabbing his coat and throwing it over his arm. He snapped out of the spell that Cynthia had on him. As Austin walked out, he turned and said, "It was really nice talking to you Cynthia. It really was." "Yes, it was Austin," Cynthia replied. They both were trying to get away from the weird vibe that they had going. Austin turned to walk away when Cynthia called his name. "Austin?" He turned and looked back at Cynthia. He shook his head, confirming that she was not wrong about the feeling she was having. Austin finally walked out of the bar. Austin called Vicky on his way home. She was worried and wondered where he had been since they had not spoken since four p.m. Austin explained that he got held up at the bar with Joe having drinks. For that, he apologized. Meanwhile, Cynthia left the bar to head home. She thought to herself, "I just made myself look as bad as Vicky." She felt ashamed. When she approached her car, Cynthia noticed a black leather wallet on the ground. When she opened the wallet, she seen it was Austin's license and business cards. It listed his cell and work numbers. Getting into her car, Cynthia thought about driving around and dropping the wallet off to Joe. Then she thought, "Damn, I did just make myself look like a fool, maybe I should just give Austin his wallet in person and apologize for my actions." Undecided, Cynthia pulled off and headed towards the bar. Arriving at the bar,

Cynthia thought once more how foolish she looked earlier. That caused her to debate more about what she should do with the wallet. Struggling to come up with a decision, Cynthia heard beeps coming from oncoming traffic in the back of her. Frustrated, she pulled off, still thinking of how she would get the wallet back to Austin. She thought, "I'll just contact Austin and meet him at the bar tomorrow." Cynthia arrived at home, trying to think of a good time to call Austin. Especially with him being married. Things could go from bad to worse if Austin's wife answered the phone. Cynthia came up with the perfect plan. She would act as if she was interested in Austin's work if his wife answered. Cynthia got herself together for the night. She bathed, oiled and relaxed in bed. Soon she fell into a deep sleep. Hours passed as the moonlight turned into the morning sunrise. Austin's alarm went off. He struggled to get out of bed due to a slight hangover. Ten minutes after the alarm went off, Austin finally made his way into the bathroom. He turned on the shower, steamed up the bathroom, and popped two Excedrin. Hopping in the shower with hopes of getting rid of his partial hangover, Austin thought about Cynthia. "Damn, that was a crazy night," he thought to himself. Then he thought, "Maybe I should mention the situation to Vicky." But Austin realized that mentioning it to Vicky, after leaving work late and going to the bar where a woman hit on him causing him to come home late, was not the best idea. He decided not to tell Vicky. He finished up in the shower, dried off, and headed to the bedroom. "Good morning baby," Vicky said as Austin walked in. "Good morning beautiful," Austin said walking over and giving Vicky a kiss on the lips. "You didn't have to work early today?" Austin asked. "No baby, I'm going in at my normal time. I'll be busy next week though." "Oh ok, cool. I have something planned for you this evening," Austin said as he smiled. "Oh really?" "Yeah, really. I'll send you the details later baby." Vicky raised her eyebrows with excitement on her face. "I can't wait to see what you've come up with baby." Vicky said. Walking over to the closet Austin said "I'm sure it's worth the wait." He picked up his jacket, from off of the floor, in search of his wallet. He realized it was not in his pocket. "Vicky, have you seen my wallet?" "No baby, maybe you left it in the car, along with your phone. That's what you were saying last night." "What do you mean?" Austin asked. Mimicking Austin, "Well you was like 'aw babe... My fucking phone is in the car. Can you go get it?' And I told your drunk ass no. And you was like 'oh, I love you anyway. I'll get it in the morning.'" "I don't sound like that," Austin said. He laughed as he threw on some clothes to go grab his phone. He prayed that his wallet was there too. Austin opened up the door and found his phone. He searched all around the interior, edges, cracks, and corners for his wallet, but he found nothing. Getting out the car, Austin said, "Shit! I knew I shouldn't have been fucking around with Joe." Walking back in the house, he yelled to Vicky, "I think I left my wallet at the bar. I have to go check for it." "That's what your drunk ass gets," Vicky said, laughing at Austin as he rushed to put his suit on. He finished getting dressed and rushed back to his car and headed to the bar. Trying to decide if he should call his credit card companies to cancel them, Austin picked up his phone and noticed that he had a voicemail. Curious, Austin played the voicemail. "Hey, I'm not sure if you remember me, but my name is Cynthia. I ran into you and your friend at Lowe's a week or two ago. I was in the process of looking for a contractor and I literally stumbled over you." Cynthia laughed. "What I meant by that was, I stumbled over your wallet on the side walk. I recognized your face and seen your business number and figured I'd give you a call. Please call me when you get a chance." In shock and caught off guard, Austin immediately called Cynthia back. She picked up. "Hello?" "Umm, Hi. I'm glad you have my wallet. I was hoping I could come and get it from you while it's still early." Austin said. Cynthia sounding as if she was in a rush. "Yeah, that's why I called you early this morning, but I'm currently about to go in a very important meeting." Austin sighs in frustration. "Well, is there a way I could come to your office and get it?" "I'm sorry, but I'm going to be in this meeting for at least 2 to 3 hours. How about I meet you at the bar? That way I could get some food after work and apologize for my actions in person." Cynthia suggested. "I don't mean to be rude or seem as if I'm mad. I do know you doing me a favor, but why can't you leave it at your front desk? I mean, how am I supposed to eat today?" Austin asked. Still rushing, Cynthia said, "Austin you are a big boy. You will figure it out. I have to go. Meet you at the bar around the same time." Cynthia hung up the phone. Frustrated, Austin threw his phone on the seat. He thought, " how the hell am I going to get out of this mess. Austin wanted to call Thomas and tell him what was going on. But he knew Thomas would feel funny about him talking to Cynthia. That would make things worse, so he kept it to himself. Austin arrived at work and headed straight to his office, avoiding his usual three minute morning meeting with his front desk employee, Peter. Austin did not even stop to say, "good-morning." in the break room. Nor did he grab his glazed donut like he usually would. His main focus was how to get to his wallet. He prayed to God that Vicky did not make dinner plans for them. Prayed harder that she would not want to have lunch. As Austin sat in his office, driving himself crazy, he called Joe to let him know everything that had just happened. Being the non-stressful person Joe was, he informed Austin to calm down. Joe told Austin, "If Cynthia wants to meet you, just meet her and get the wallet. If there were any other problems that came up, like Vicky wanting to do lunch or dinner, just tell Vicky you simply didn't find your wallet and maybe it's with Joe at the bar." Finally Austin started to calm down. Joe made sense of things and convinced Austin that things were not as bad as he was making them out to be. Austin got off the phone and went out into the lobby. Now, he was able to go through his daily routine. A few hours passed when Austin received a text from Vicky. She asked him what his plans were for lunch. Austin immediately went into a minor panic attack. Then he remembered what Joe said and became calm. Austin replied, "Well baby, I'm going to get some food delivered. Kind of busy at the office today." Vicky was excited to hear that Austin was staying in the office. Her text was just to cover her tracks so she could tell Mr. Smith that she would be free for lunch. Vicky replied, "Aww babe. Lunch would have been great today but I'll let you focus, my sexy man. Love you." Relieved, Austin text back, "Yeah, babe it would have been. I guess I'll see you tonight at home, and I love you too." "Ok," Vicky sent back, smiling mischievously on the other end of the phone. During the time Vicky was texting, Cynthia walked past Vicky, asking what her plans were for lunch. Vicky smiled. Cynthia asked, "Mr. Smith?" Vicky nodded her head yes, while still smiling. Then Vicky asked, "Girl, why you been looking lost today? What's on your mind?" Cynthia did not want to consult with Vicky, but she had no one else, so she told her. "I kind of came on to a married man last night." Vicky smiled and said, "Girl, I'm rubbing off on you already!" Not feeling the compliment, Cynthia slightly smile and said, "No, I don't need to be doing that." Vicky asked, "Girl, why not? A married man is like a secret service penis. That's a gift wrapped from God. I'm talking, Men in Black kind of secrets." "What?" Cynthia asked. "You heard me." Vicky said. "The feeling of it being wrong will make the sex that much better. Especially if it's good from the start. Oh, and don't let me forget to mention, they don't kiss and tell. Too much to lose." "I don't want to be involved in that Victoria. I mean, what if we were to get caught? Then he would lose out on his family and even some friends. Some people to people relationships are more important than just fucking. Don't you sometimes feel bad? Is the pleasure worth the bad that comes if you got mix up with all that bullshit?" Cynthia asked. Vicky looked at Cynthia and said, "Girl that sounded like me a few years ago. See that's why you just find you one person and stick with them and be up front and that way you won't have to worry about being in a bunch of bullshit." Cynthia smirked and looked at Vicky. "So you're just fucking Mr. Smith, no feeling nor emotions have ever revealed themselves if he had to cancel on you? You didn't feel bad at all?" Cynthia asked as she started to walk off. Vicky followed Cynthia and said, "Yeah, it happened before and I almost blew my marriage." "So why do it again?" Cynthia asked. Vicky ignored Cynthia's question and asked her, "What's your favorite season?" Cynthia smiled and said, "That's random, but fall. It's so nice and beautiful how the trees come together making this 'home comfort' color with their leaves. I'll tell you Vicky, it's nothing like a cup of hot chocolate on a cold fall day." Vicky smiled. "I wasn't thinking a girl from Miami would say that." Cynthia laughed "I used to visit my grandparents in North Carolina and I miss that feeling." Vicky said "Now, that's what I mean. That feeing you have when you're missing something. See, Cynthia, I love my husband. But being around him makes me miss Mr. Smith and when I'm with Mr. Smith, I miss my husband. They play a role. I know I should not be with Mr. Smith. But it's that bad sex, rough and outgoing feeling I get when I'm with him. But sometimes it can be too much. Then I get home with my husband and I get that home sweet home feeling. That simple but perfect life. Dinner cooked, bath ran and feet rubbed type of thing. I just feel like, why enjoy one season, once a year when you can make your favorite season work for you year round." Vicky made cheating seem right. Cynthia still disagreed, but played it off. "Yeah, I guess you're right." "See you get me." Vicky said. Then Vicky asked, "Well, what this married man look like? Is he fine?" Cynthia replied, "Girl, is he! He is the definition of fine." "Well, let me see him? Does he have a Facebook?" Cynthia paused and said, "Now that I think about it, I have a picture of him in my office." "Well, if he's that fine and excites you that much, I guess it's worth the walk to your office." Cynthia tried to down play the situation as she took notice she was going down the wrong path. She tried to tell Vicky she would show her another day, but Vicky was being nosy and she insisted. "Girl, come on and let me see this chocolate man you're trying to hide." "Well, ok." Cynthia said as the ladies made their way, giggling like two school girls. As they headed towards the elevator, Vicky's phone went off. It was Mr. Smith, telling her he was outside. She quickly canceled the mission with Cynthia and Cynthia was relieved. Cynthia made her way to her office. She decided to skip lunch and just snack, while she planned a business solution for an upcoming project. Time had flown by and it was time for her to go home. Cynthia looked at her phone. There were a few missed text messages from Austin. Cynthia figured she would lock up her office and just call Austin when she got in her car. On the elevator, Cynthia ran into Vicky. "Hey girl." Vicky said. Not trying to bring up the picture of her married man, Cynthia quickly said, "Girl, I can't wait until I can get out these heels." Vicky laughed. "Yeah, well I been got out of mine." Referring to Mr. Smith and their sexual encounter. Cynthia replied, "Must be nice." "Now I get to go home and relax with another favorite season." Cynthia thought to herself how Vicky was such a hoe. She agreed and asked, "So what if he just hops on you when you get home?" Vicky said "Baby, I'm going to the gym to workout, for an hour, then shower. Plus, I have a small thing of KY just in case." Cynthia said, "Damn, you got it all planned out huh?" "Yes, I do. And if you want this married man of yours, I can teach you how to get him." Cynthia responded, "No, I'll pass. But if I want him, I know who to come to." When the elevator door opened, the women walked off and started going their separate ways. Before they gained some distance, Cynthia turned around and called for Vicky. Vicky turned and said, "What's up?" Cynthia said, "I really like you and I've seen some crazy shit happen to people. Just make sure you are being careful with all that stuff." "I got it girl," Vicky said. Cynthia looked at Vicky as if she was looking through her. "Vicky, just remember. Every season has rain, beware of the storms." Vicky's smile turned into a frown as Cynthia turned around and walked off. "Cynthia!" Vicky yelled. Cynthia stopped and turned around. Vicky said, "Thank you. No one has ever been bold enough to be honest with me. Especially with me being their boss." "You got it" Cynthia said as she made her way through the doors. Getting in her car, Cynthia called Austin. He answered, "Hello?" "Hey, are you at the bar?" Cynthia asked. "No, I'm just finishing up at work. I'm leaving literally in like five minutes." "Ok, well I live like ten minutes from the bar, I'm going to run home and let my dog out." Cynthia said. "Ok. Can you please make sure you are there when I get there in thirty minutes? I'm not trying to get caught up in any more games." Said Austin. "Sure, but I'm not playing any games. I wanted you to know that I was one hundred percent wrong for what I did last night. And I wanted you to know I'm not like that nor do I plan on tricking you into anything." Cynthia explained. "Ok, I get it. But can't you tell your brother to let the dog out and you just wait for me?" Austin asked. "I don't have a brother. You think I was supposed to tell two men, that I don't know, that I've move to Richmond by myself?" Cynthia asked. "Well, you were meeting a contractor you didn't know." "I was meeting him yes, but he worked with my father and had just moved up here, so my father reached out to him," she explained. "Well anyways..." Austin said, feeling dumb, "...Just be there on time please." They both agreed to be there in thirty minutes. Cynthia got home to let her dog out. On the way back to her car, she noticed she had a flat tire. Thinking to herself, she thought if she was to call Austin, he would definitely think this was planned. But she had no one else to call. Cynthia reached to call Austin but he was already calling her. Cynthia picked up. "Hey Austin," she said as her voice raised suspension. Austin immediately caught onto Cynthia's voice and asked, "What now?" "I have a flat tire." Austin exhaled and said, "Well, give me your address and I'll send an Uber." Cynthia said, "What the fuck Austin? I'm not fucking twenty-one and I'm not trying to get a late night creep. Look I don't know how to change it. You don't even have to come in my house or anything. Can you just change my tire, I will fucking pay you!" Cynthia shouted in frustration. Feeling bad, Austin said, "Look, just text me your address and I'll come change your tire." "Thank you for being a man. A grown man. And I am about to send you the address." She hung up. It did not take long before Austin was pulling up to Cynthia's house. He was amazed that a single woman like Cynthia was living by herself in such a big house. Her house was two stories with gray brick stone on the outside. The red door matched the red rosebush she had trailing the front. The mulch was placed perfectly along the neatly trimmed grass. Austin thought, "Yeah, she must have had a good contractor." Cynthia was walking out her house as Austin was getting out the car. "Hey."

Cynthia spoke, walking towards Austin. Austin spoke back and asked, "Do you have my wallet?" "Oh no you don't. I'm not giving you your wallet until you change my tire." Austin said, "I have on a Thirty-five hundred dollar suit." Cynthia responded, "If you can afford it, I know you have more of them at home." She hit the trunk release button on her key. Austin sighed as he walked over to her car, took out the tire and oily four iron. Looking at Cynthia, Austin asked, "Really?" She started laughing as she noticed the oil. "I'm sorry, I didn't know." Austin handed Cynthia his suit jacket and got under the car to start changing the tire. In no time, the tire was off. Austin found out what caused the tire to go flat. "Thanks." Cynthia said as she tossed Austin his wallet. "It sure was nice having a man around the house." The two made eye contact for a slit second and Cynthia burst out laughing. "I'm joking, Austin. Cheer up and find some humor." Austin chuckle a little. "Yeah, I know, but I honestly didn't know if you was joking or not." They both laughed some more as Austin put the tools back in the trunk. When doing that he cut his hand on an open blade, Austin yelled out, "Shit!" "Oh my God, are you ok?" Cynthia asked while rushing over to look at Austin's hand. "Maybe, maybe not." When Cynthia saw the cut and the blood, she led Austin into her house. As he walked into her house, he noticed how good it smelled. Her marble floors were nice and neat. Austin started checking out each room as he went down the hallway. He noticed how every room held a different vibe. The walls were freshly painted but were still out lined with blue tape. Some rooms were furnished but not all the way in order. Cynthia led Austin to the island in the middle of the kitchen where the kitchen sink was located. Applying pressure to Austin's hand, Cynthia said, "My sister is a nurse back home. She showed me how to bandage someone up from a bad cut." "Is this a real sister? Not like the brother you had?" Austin asked. Cynthia laugh and asked, "So you have to get cut in order to find your sense of humor huh? And for your information. Yes, she is my real sister." Austin switched the conversation and asked, "So what are you doing with all this house? I mean, I wasn't expecting you to have such a big house. Especially being that you are alone." "You weren't expecting my house to be big, or are you intimidated that I'm a woman that has this amazing house?" "No, no I'm not bias nor am I intimidated. I just was thinking. A nice house like this is more so a family house." When Austin said that, Cynthia poured rubbing alcohol on his deeply wounded hand. "Damn, that shit stings. Watch how much you put on there!" Austin shouted with pain in his voice. Ignoring Austin's request, Cynthia poured more on. "I have to get the germs out," She said with a little attitude. He picked up on the change of tone and vibe with Cynthia. Austin asked, "What's the problem? Why all of a sudden did you get mad when I mentioned a family?" As Austin finished his sentence, he remembered that Cynthia's ex-husband cheated on her. "Oh shit, I'm sorry," Austin said, leaning his back on the island as Cynthia dropped Austin's hand. "No, it's ok." Cynthia responded as her facial expression held back pain. "Look, I truly didn't mean to bring it up." Cynthia wrapped Austin's hand up. "It's ok I said, but I think it's time for you to go. You have your wallet. I'll show you the way to the door." He followed Cynthia, feeling guilty. The two quietly arrived at the front door and Cynthia said, "I really appreciate you changing my tire. I don't know how I would have gotten to work in the morning." Austin smiled. "Well, you could have just asked that creepy old guy that was watering his grass to help you." Cynthia smiled "Stop talking about Mr. Butch." as she gave Austin a little push on the arm. "Lord knows, he would have love to have helped me though." They both laughed, but Austin seen that Cynthia was still down. "Look..." Cynthia cut him off "Stop, just go." "No, you need to hear this. Cynthia. I'm terrified of you." "What?" she asked. Austin repeated, "I'm terrified of you. I'm a married man. I've been one happily married man for a long time now. I never cheated. I love, respect and cherish my wife. But you terrify me because the other night, I seen myself with you. Now I get here and you're standing right in front of me. Looking beautiful and you're not even trying. I mean, you have your own and you're looking for what I have to offer. Not saying you're looking for me, but someone like me. And to know that you're hurting because someone cheated on you... that's messed up. I been down that road and I know deep inside that if I hadn't stayed strong, I would have met you and we would have been together. That terrifies me." Cynthia stood in shock, emotionless. She just stared at Austin as if she understood and felt exactly what he was saying. Cynthia bit her lip as she looked down at the ground. Slowly lifting her head while a tear fell down her face. Austin stepped towards Cynthia and grabbed her face, wiping the tear with his thumb. "I'm terrified to risk you." Cynthia, inhaled quickly as she looked down at the ground once more while grabbing Austin's hand. Looking up, Cynthia exhaled softly, making eye contact with

Austin. Cynthia spoke and softly said, "I'm not here to make you risk anything because it wouldn't be a risk. There would be no danger in my love." Relieved but afraid, Austin sighed as he was speechless. Before the two could say anymore, Austin's phone rung. It was Vicky. "Just go, please just go." Cynthia said while pushing Austin out of the door. Austin walked away. He turned around, not believing what had just happened. Austin got into his car and pulled off to call Vicky.

Chapter 5.

"Hello?" Vicky asked as she picked up the phone. "Hey baby. I missed your call." Austin replied with a broken voice. "Are you ok? You sound a little weird." She asked. "Yeah, I'm just a little shaken up. This car swerved in front me and I almost crashed. I just got out of traffic safe and sound though." "Oh my god! I'm glad you're ok baby." Clearing his throat he said. "I'll be fine. It just was a close one. But it's all good." "Thank goodness. Hey, I remembered this morning you were having a little trouble finding your wallet. Did you ever find it?" She asked. "My wallet! Umm yeah, yeah. It was with Joe behind the bar." "Why are you so jumpy about your wallet?" She asked. Lying threw his teeth he answered. "Oh, I was just trying to figure out where I put it after I got it from Joe. No big deal. I remembered. It's in the armrest." Trying to avoid the whole wallet conversation, he quickly changed the subject and asked. "Where are you coming from babe?" "Oh, I'm just leaving the gym. I had a great workout. I was all sweaty and everything. I had to take a shower there." She replied. "Damn, I was hoping you hadn't taken a shower yet. I would have loved to hop in the shower behind that ass and mount you like a horse." He said as Vicky laughed. "Oh you feeling nasty huh, baby?" With confidence Austin said, "Baby I feel nasty, freaky or whatever you want to call it. "You giving me a piece of that ass?'" "Well, I'll be sure to have a nice treat for you Mr. Roberts." She said. Excited and horny Austin yelled, "I can't wait to see what you have in mind!" "Yeah, it's going to be a good treat. I'm sure you'll like it. Now let me get off this phone and figure it out. I'm pulling up to the house. I'll see you when you get here." She said. "Sure thing baby. I'll see you soon." Austin replied as they both hung up. He was guilt tripping because he still had Cynthia on his mind. Feeling bad about what happened, Austin told himself that he had to stay away from Cynthia. So he began to block Cynthia out of his head and kept his focus on his wife. Austin arrived at his house. He got his thoughts together before he made his way to the door. When he walked in the house he smelled dinner cooking and heard the shower running. He walked down the hallway, searching. "Vicky! Where you at, girl?" Austin called out. As he approached the bedroom, he was disappointed when he found Vicky. He thought she would be in something sexy. Instead she had on a nice pair of dark blue jeans that grabbed her curves and a black tank top that read SOZA down the middle. "That's my treat." He asked before walking towards and grabbing her. He then looked in her eye and said. "I fucking love you." "I love you too." She said. "Well I'm guessing I'm on time for my treat." Austin said with a smile. "What you mean?" She asked confused. "My treat. You said you was giving me a treat. My guess is that dinner is already cooking. You have the shower running for me and I just have to be patient and wait for the main event tonight." Vicky looked at Austin a started laughing. "Well, that sounds like a plan, but your daughter is in the shower. Which means I didn't run the shower for you and Patrick is coming over for dinner. So dinner isn't just for you either. It's for everybody. And it won't be ready until everyone is ready. And sorry to tell you, but as far as your main event, my legs are cramping from the gym. So that's not happening either." Vicky said with a slight frown.

Upset, Austin asked, "Jasmine's here? I didn't even see her car. How did she get here? Hell, how did she get in the house?" "Well, she is our daughter and she grew up in this house. So my guess is that she used her key when Patrick dropped her off. Oh, and speaking of Patrick. When he dropped her off, he said he is going to propose tonight!" "What!" Austin said. "She still has a key? What if I was walking around the house naked. Ass naked, relaxing in my house. I'm taking her key back." Vicky said, "First of all, you are not going to take her key. That's what you always say. Second of all, did you not hear me? Patrick is going to propose to your one and only daughter tonight at dinner. You need to stop being such an angry, horny man all the time." Austin said, "Yeah whatever." as he walked away from Vicky. He made his way to the foot of the bed to take off his shoes. "I already told him yeah, what else you want me to do? I thought the boy would have been did the whole proposal thing. But if he wants to do it here, I guess I'll have to attend dinner." Vicky responded. "You were going to attend dinner anyway, even if he wasn't proposing with your hungry ass. The next best thing to sex with you is eating. I'll give you that honey. You do find some good restaurants." "Yeah, food is life." Austin said, as Jasmine entered the room in her towel. "Oh, daddy!" Jasmine yelled trying to cover up her body. "See Vicky. This what I'm talking about. She walking around, half naked, relaxing herself in my house but I can't even do that because she has a key." Vicky and Jasmine started laughing as Austin walked out of the room. He then yelled, "Jasmine, I need the key to your house before you leave." "Why?" Jasmine asked. "So I can walk around your house naked like you walk around mine." Jasmine frowned her face up. "No, daddy that's just nasty." Austin mumbled under his breath. "Your nasty ass all up in my house, in my towel. Go home." Vicky and Jasmine laughed once more as Austin complained about not having freedom in his own house. Deep down inside, Austin liked having his daughter around and like having something to complain about. He made his way to the kitchen, grabbed a spoon and started snooping around to see what was done cooking. As he began to pull back the foil, he heard Vicky yell, "Austin, you better keep your hands out of my pots!" "I'm not in your pots." He lifted the aluminum foil, digging into the mac and cheese. Austin grabbed a beer out the fridge and sat on the new recliner to kick his feet up. As soon as he got comfortable, his phone went off. He was relieved to see it was not Cynthia. Rather, it was his right hand man, Thomas, sending him a text. "What up. I need to talk to you about that girl I told you I loved." Before he could reply, Jasmine walked in the room smiling. "Is this better daddy?" As she pointed out she was fully dressed. "Yeah, I guess." Austin said still pretending to be mad. Jasmine walked into the kitchen. "Daddy, mom is going to kill you." "Huh?" Austin yelled out. "You dug in her mac and cheese." "See, no. That wasn't me." Austin said. "Well, if it wasn't you. Are you being framed with that cheese on your chin." "What you mean?" He asked feeling for the cheese on his chin. "You better go get it off before mom sees it." Jasmines said laughing. Before he left the kitchen to head to the bathroom he asked Jasmine. "Are you going to get a little mac and cheese with me?" "No, stop trying to drag me down with you!" She replied laughing. "Now hurry up. Mom is coming and she's going to kill you when she sees that cheese on your chin now. Go!" They both laughed as Austin rushed to the bathroom. He saw the cheese on his chin and grabbed some tissue to wipe it off. He threw the tissue in the trashcan when he noticed something that looked like a broken tampon wrapped in tissue. Austin paid it no mind as he hopped in the shower. Shortly after Austin began to wash up, he heard Vicky banging on the door and yelling. "I told your ass to stay out my pots." Austin started laughing. "I didn't. The mac and cheese was in a pan." "You knew what I meant when I said that Austin!" Vicky yelled. Austin started laughing some more. Vicky said, "You're lucky this is a special night because your black ass wouldn't be eating. Oh, and there goes your main event for tomorrow night." She yelled. Austin's face quickly turned from a joyful smile to a frown. He thought to himself. "What do I have to do to get some ass round here?" Austin finished washing up and stepped out of the shower. He saw, what appeared to be, a corner of a box with a half ripped number two on it. Under the two, it read, "Test." Austin immediately dug through the trash. His heart dropped as he seen the balled up tissue. Austin grabbed it and unwrapped the tissue. There, he held a Clearblue pregnancy test. In shock, Austin sat on the edge of the tub wondering, "How long has Vicky known she was pregnant and why didn't she say anything." He did not understand, but he knew for sure he would get to the bottom of it. Austin quickly dried off, grabbed his shirt and pants off the floor, and marched into his bedroom. Right behind him stood Vicky. Before she could say anything, Austin turned and asked in a low angry voice, "So we keeping secrets now? We doing things

90

behind each other's back?" Shocked, Vicky automatically went into a defense. "I don't know what you're talking about!" Inside, Vicky was terrified and praying that Austin did not find out about Mr. Smith. "Don't play stupid. We had this conversation before." Still down playing things, Vicky said, "Baby, I have no idea what you are talking." Vicky noticed Austin had his phone in his hand. She asked, "What are you talking about Austin? You're holding your phone like you found something." "What?" Austin asked as he threw his phone on the bed. "No, it's nothing on there. But it was something in the trash." Confused, Vicky asked, "The trash?" Calming down, Austin said, "Yeah Vicky, the trash. You're pregnant and you weren't going to tell me. I thought we had got everything fixed. If you were trying to get pregnant again, you should have told me right away." So relived, so happy and so satisfied that she wasn't caught, Vicky belted out into laughter. "What are you laughing at?" Austin asked. "Do you remember how much of a wreck you were and how you were going crazy when I told you I was pregnant with Jas?" Vicky asked. "Yeah. I remember. Why?" Austin asked as he started smiling a little. "That's how you're acting now. In shock. Excited, but scared out your mind. Baby, that definitely is not my test. But, that can only mean one thing. We're having a grandbaby!" Vicky said with excitement. "Hush, hush, hush, Jas doesn't know that we know. She's probably going to say something after Patrick proposes tonight." "Oh this is so exciting!" Vicky said full of joy. Austin sat down on the bed, happy to know that he was going to be a grandpa. He looked and Vicky. "Baby, I'm sorry." Vicky walked over to him. "Baby, there's no need to be sorry. I

91

know your happy dance sometimes misses a beat, but I'm not pregnant. I'll get everything that comes with a baby, just without the morning sickness. And you'll get everything, just without the big pressure of being a new father." "Yeah. You're right baby." The doorbell sounded. Vicky said, "That's Patrick. Let the excitement begin." Vicky then kissed Austin on the lips and headed to the front door. Austin got dressed as his excitement grew. He headed down to meet everyone when his phone went off again. It was Thomas texting him. "Yo, you want to meet me at a bar?" Austin replied back. "Doing dinner with the family. Patrick's proposing tonight." Walking in the kitchen, Austin sat his phone down to greet Patrick. "Hey Patrick. How are you doing today?" Patrick got up from the couch and walked over to Austin. "Hey, what up Mr. Roberts?" Patrick asked, sticking his hand out. Austin grabbed Patrick's hand, pulling him close. "So I hear tonight's the night. You know I love my daughter. Now don't you disappoint me in the future! I will feel bad if I made the wrong decision and I will have to take it out on someone. Understand, I won't be killing myself. If you get what I'm saying. Now welcome to the family." Austin said, as he released Patrick from his grips. Nervously, Patrick said, "Yeah, I know what you mean Mr. Roberts." Vicky walked into the kitchen looking at Austin and Patrick as if she knew what had just happened. Right away, she spoke softly while looking at the two men. "You better not be threatening that boy, Austin." "I wasn't doing no such thing. Was I Patrick?" Clearing his throat, Patrick said, "No, no, nothing of that matter Mrs. V." "Yeah, I hear you. Now come on and let's get this food in our bellies. I know that one is hungry." Vicky said while looking at Austin.

Vicky and Patrick walked off as Austin followed saying, "You damn right I'm hungry. I have to wait to eat in my own house. Shit. Patrick, you're saying the grace." They all sat down at the dining room table where the food was laid out. There were four big steaks, mac and cheese, fresh string beans and warm cornbread with a side salad. Vicky also had a cheesecake for dessert that was sitting on the side waiting to be devoured. Jasmine said, "I knew you were making dinner but wow, this is a bit much. You only cook like this for special occasions." "This is one." She said, as Austin and Patrick looked at Vicky. Both thinking, "don't you blow it." Vicky quickly said, "Our family is together. We never eat like this in the house unless it's a cookout. I just wanted us to enjoy a nice dinner." "Yeah, you're right mom." "Yeah she's right, now can you two let Patrick bless the food so we can eat like it's a cookout?" Austin asked. They all laughed and Patrick asked if everyone would bow their heads as he said grace. "Heavenly father, we thank you for the food we're about to receive. We ask you to bless the hands that prepared it. In Jesus name we pray, amen." Amen everyone said. All four of them, held conversations, shared laughs, and enjoyed one another's company, as they feasted like a happy family on Thanksgiving. Once they all finished eating, Vicky said, "Jas. Go and get a knife so we can cut the cheesecake." "Ok." Jasmine said with a full stomach, slowly moving towards the kitchen. When Jasmine left, Vicky asked, "Patrick, are you ready?" Nervously, Patrick responded. "I think so." "You think so?" Austin asked. "You need to know because here she comes." As Jasmine came into the dining room to sit down, Patrick stood up and looked at Austin. Austin smiled and nodded. Patrick then looked at Jasmine. "Baby, my past is not the best and I've done a lot of wrong, but I've corrected my mistakes. I started out having no money, which quickly changed to me having a lot of money. In the process, I almost had my life taken away from me. Through everything, I realized you were always important to me. I knew that if I didn't drop all of my childish behaviors, I would have been risking you and I could have potentially lost you. You kept me from turning into what people thought I was going to be, and helped me mold into someone I never thought I could be. With your help, I found myself. With your help, I've change for the best. I didn't graduate high school, I have a GED and that was because of you. And now I've turn that GED into a Doctrine. So Jasmine Roberts, with your help, I want to be the best husband I can be." Patrick dropped on one knee and pulled out a two carat, round, colorless center diamond in a 14k white gold setting. He looked Jasmine in her eyes and asked, "Jasmine Roberts. Will you marry me?" Already with a face full of tears, Jasmine said, "Yes! Yes, I'll marry you Patrick!" The two smiled with teary eyes as they hugged one another. Austin hugged Vicky as if he was the one getting married. Vicky ran over to Patrick and Jasmine, hugging them both. Austin rushed into the kitchen to get the bottle of 1958 cabernet wine and four glasses. He called for everyone to sit down. He popped the cork on the wine and poured the aged cabernet into everyone's glass. "Allow me to make a toast." Austin said as he handed everyone a glass of wine. "To my new son in-law and to my daughter. I wish you both the best in your marriage. There will be rough times and it will be hard, but remember to stay strong. Cheers." Before everyone glasses could hit together, Vicky said. "Austin, let's not forget about our new grandbaby that is on the way." Everyone's glasses hit and they all took a sip. Patrick said, "Yeah, a baby. I can't wait. The future holds so much for us and I can't wait until we decide to have one." Austin realized that Patrick did not know that Jasmine was pregnant. Vicky missed that message as she was still full of excitement. Austin tried kicking Vicky's foot to get her attention but he hit the table instead. Vicky blurted out, "So Jasmine, how far along are you? Your dad and I found the test." Patrick choked a little from sipping his wine and looked at Jasmine. "You're pregnant?" Patrick asked. Austin looked at Jasmine and saw something was not right. Patrick smirked. "This is unbelievable, you're pregnant?" Vicky said, "Yes. You better believe it. You're going to be father." Austin seen Patrick's face. It looked as if he was numb, but outraged at the same time. Patrick stood up. "Mr. and Mrs. Roberts, unfortunately, I am not a father nor am I going to be one. You see, Jasmine is not on birth control and she also didn't want us to get pregnant until we were ready. She forced me to wear condoms every time we had sex for the last six months. With all due respect, I damn sure don't have a one year old kid nor is Jasmine six months pregnant." He laughed in heartbreak. Vicky realized what she had done. Looking at Jasmine, whose happy tears had turned into depressed tears. Patrick looked down at Jasmine as she wilt in tears. "Jasmine, I won't be marrying you." Patrick tried to walk away from the table but Jasmine grabbed his arm screaming out. "I'm sorry Patrick! I'm so sorry Patrick! Baby wait, please forgive me!" By this time, Vicky and

Austin were standing up trying to gain control of the situation. Patrick was still trying to leave and Jasmine continued to try and stop him. Searching for the right words to say, Austin grabbed Patrick and Vicky grabbed Jasmine. They pulled the two apart. Patrick leaned over, placing his forehead on the wall as he broke down in tears. He screamed out, "I gave her my all Mr. Roberts! I gave her my all!" The doorbell rang as Austin rubbed Patrick's back. "I know, you just have to be strong. You got this far in life being strong son." The doorbell sounded again. Austin said, "Patrick, I have to get the door. Stay right here." Austin rushed to the door. It was Thomas. "Yo, what up?" Thomas asked. "What up? Look, come in. Some crazy shit just happen with Patrick and Jasmine." "Do I need to fuck him up?" "Your odds of winning right now are low, so chill. It's not the time to play." Austin said. Thomas and Austin walked in the house, as they got close to the kitchen, they could hear Patrick yelling with rage. "Who's baby is it Jasmine? You had to be fucking someone to get pregnant." Austin entered first, telling Patrick to calm down while trying to get him outside. When Thomas entered the kitchen, Jasmine's face turned pale and her eyes got wide. Jasmine made eye contact with Thomas. Vicky saw all that just happened. She immediately thought she knew who had gotten Jasmine pregnant. She knew that if Austin was to find out, he would kill Thomas dead in their kitchen. Everyone was yelling over each other as Austin tried to calm Patrick down. Patrick noticed that Jasmine and Thomas were both in shock. He screamed out over Austin and asked." Really? Really Jas? Thomas? Thomas got Jasmine pregnant Austin!" The kitchen got quiet. Austin looked at

Patrick and said, "Now you're crossing the line. Patrick you're wrong." With red teary eyes, Patrick looked at Thomas and calmly said, "I'm going to fuck you up. You're going to wish that you've never crossed me." "Enough!" Austin yelled. "Let me take you to your car. Avoid any bars tonight, you don't want to do anything stupid and fuck up everything you have accomplished over emotions." Austin walked Patrick to the door. Patrick looked at Thomas again with rage in his eyes. Patrick left peacefully. When Austin walked back into the kitchen, everyone was still standing in the same spot. "What the fuck is going on? ...Jasmine, who is this fucker who got you pregnant?... Thomas, you see this shit? All this fucking drama in my house. Who got you pregnant Jasmine?" Jasmine didn't say anything and stormed out the kitchen. Austin followed Jasmine and yelled "Where are you going? You didn't drive." Jasmine walked outside and sat on the porch. Vicky followed her, telling Austin to back off. Austin walked in the kitchen to grab two beers. He handed Thomas a beer. "I can't even imagine how that boy is feeling." Austin said. "Yeah. Maybe she loves the other guy Austin." Thomas said. "Yeah maybe. It's not right, but love is love you know." "Yeah, I do." Thomas said. Thomas than sipped his beer and looked out of the front door at Vicky and Jasmine. "But anyway, what did you have to tell me about this girl you are so called 'in love with?'" Austin asked with a chuckle. "Well, she's pregnant." Thomas said. "What?" "T, you're having a baby?" "Yeah man, I guess I am. But I don't know if she going to keep it though." "See that's what you get for messing with them hoes." Thomas looked at Austin and said, "This one is not a hoe. We just happened to happen,

97

you know." "Yeah man. I get it. Love comes when it wants to." "What's her name?" Thomas got quiet and looked outside at Jasmine. "Thomas, what's her name?" Thomas still was looking at Jasmine and said, "Austin, I need to tell you something." "What up T? Spit it out." Thomas looked at Austin and said, "Jasmine is who I love and who I got pregnant." Austin paused. Then he chuckled a little and asked, "My Jasmine?" Thomas started to blink, his eyes fighting tears. Looking down to the floor Thomas whispered. "I'm sorry A." Thomas looked up but before he could get another word out. Austin took his beer bottle and smashed it on the right side of Thomas' face. Cutting him above his cheek bone. Before the rest of the bottle hit the floor, Austin had punched Thomas and connected with his left jaw, causing him to hit the floor. Thomas blurted out. "Sorry! I'm sorry. I fucked up Austin." Vicky heard the thumping and yelling in the house. She ran as Austin was kicking Thomas in the ribs, fracturing two of them. "Stop Austin! Stop!" Vicky yelled as he picked up a marble vase and smashed it on Thomas's knee. Thomas tried to cover his wounded body. Vicky tried to hop in front of Austin as he headed to the bedroom to get his gun. Vicky pulled and screamed in terror, trying to stop Austin. He dragged her along as Vicky was no match for Austin. He made it to the bedroom, punched in the code to unlock his safe and reached for his gun. There was a loud slam! He looked up and Vicky had slammed the bedroom door and locked it. Vicky then took her high school baton and broke the nob off of the door, locking Austin and herself in the room. She yelled out, "Stop Austin! I love and I need you!" Austin pause. Those words were like water to a fire. "I love you." Vicky said as tears poured down her face. "How you're acting is not the person I love. Do you love me?" Austin stood there with a blank face. Then she yelled again, "Do you love me?" Taking a deep breath, Austin said, "Yes." Then he yelled out. "I love Jasmine and Thomas too. But how could they betray me like this? All these years. How could he do this to me?" "Baby, I know you're hurting, but like you just told Patrick, don't do anything stupid over emotions." Austin looked at Vicky as his rage calmed down. He threw the gun on the bed. Covered in tears, Vicky rushed over and hugged Austin. He released Vicky from his arms and made his way to the door. Taking a pen off the dresser, Austin stuck the pen in the door to turn the knob. Before he opened the door, Vicky stopped him. "I know you're mad, but if you leave out this room and do something stupid you would never be able to enjoy me, your recliner and beer anymore." Austin sighed as he looked back and smiled at Vicky. "Your meals. I'd never get another one of your meals." He finally opened the door and said, "Too bad I'm a fool for your cooking Vicky." He walked out of the bedroom and saw the mess he had made. Austin got to the front door and saw Jasmine struggling to get Thomas in his passenger seat. Austin walked outside toward the car and Jasmine stopped in fear. Austin looked at Thomas and said, "You are no longer a part of my life. Don't call, text or try to get in touch with me for any reason." Jasmine said, "Daddy, don't be like that. Thomas is your best friend." Austin snatched Jasmine keys and started taking his house key off. He said, "That goes for you too." Austin dropped Jasmine keys and started to walk to the porch. Jasmine yelled out, "Daddy! Daddy! You don't love me anymore." Austin stopped, but never looked back. Tears rolled down his face. He took a deep breath and continued to walk back in the house. He heard Jasmine ball out in tears. He walked in the house and locked his door. Going to the kitchen, he grabbed his phone off of the counter. He got a beer out of the fridge. He sat on his recliner, leaning it back, looking to relax. Moments later, his phone went off. It was Cynthia texting him. "I just need someone to vent to. No emotions, just a good talk. Do you have time?" Battling with himself, he agreed. He replied, "Be at my bar in twenty minutes." Grabbing his keys, Austin yelled to Vicky. "I'm going out to get some fresh air."

Chapter 6.

Austin pulled up to his bar. He walked in and greeted the people he knew. "What up Joe." Austin said, as he sat down beside Cynthia. "Hey Austin." Joe said. "Are you ok?" Cynthia asked, noticing Austin looked bothered. Austin didn't answer Cynthia. Instead he looked at Joe and said, "Pour a double scotch." Joe walked over and threw a glass on the bar. Then he topped it off with scotch. Joe looked at Cynthia and said, "Sweetheart, he's not going to say anything to you until he has his second double." Cynthia looked at Austin confused and asked, "Why?" "Well, other than the other night with you, Austin doesn't normally take shots unless something is wrong. And when he does, I guess he likes to get his mind right first." Cynthia looked back at Austin as he signaled Joe to pour him another double. Austin threw the double back and looked at Cynthia. "Hi." He said as if he had just seen her. "What's wrong?" Cynthia asked. "No, no you first." Austin said. Cynthia looked at Austin. "Well, I wanted to tell you about my past marriage. I've never told anyone this, but it's been on my mind." "What is it?" Austin asked. "Well..." Cynthia started, but was interrupted by Joe. "Austin, telephone!" he shouted, walking over and handing Austin the phone. "Hello?" "It's me baby. Look Austin, don't be at the bar getting drunk and can't drive home. It's been a long day and I don't want to have to come get you for a D.U.I. Nor do I want to have to see firemen scrape you off a pole." "I'm good. I'll be home soon." He said as he hung the phone up. "I can't believe this shit!" Austin yelled. "What? What's wrong Austin?" Cynthia asked. "You know you grow up with people and have their backs. Helping them the best you can and they fuck you. Cross you the first chance they get. I mean just down out disrespectful. You know people like that just makes the world a bad place Cynthia. They make it just bad." He explained. Cynthia could hear the pain in his voice. "I agree with you Austin." She said as she started feeling bad. Her concerns grew. Shifting her feet more towards Austin, she figured he needed someone to talk to a little more than she did. So, she asked. "What happened?" Looking at Cynthia and judging her loyalty to keep his secrets, he finally blurted out. "Thomas is in love with my daughter. This motherfucker got her pregnant. I can't believe it." Austin said as anger steamed out of his voice. "Oh my God! Are you kidding?" She asked. "That's who he was talking about, your daughter?" she said. "What are you talking about?" He asked. "The day I ran into Thomas. He got the talking about some girl he was in love with and how it was complicated to tell anyone." Austin twisted up his face as he looked at Cynthia. "You think this been going on for a while?" "My guess is yes, but I didn't know. Do you know how far along your daughter is?" She asked. "No, she never did say." Austin signaled for Joe to pour him another drink. He looked at his glass and said, "Cynthia, I almost killed him today." "What? Wait, he told you in person that he got your daughter pregnant?" "Yeah, he did. I was going to shoot him. I didn't know where. I just knew it was the right thing to do at the time but my wife stopped me." "Damn, I'm glad you didn't Austin. You're a good man. A nice guy. It would have been sad to see you go down because of Thomas' bullshit. You

102

must have a strong wife that cares about you alot." Cynthia softly told Austin. "Yeah. She does her part." He said, agreeing with Cynthia. "So, you had a long day I see. Not including earlier." She said as she sighed. Right then, Austin remembered that he wanted to stay away from Cynthia. Just because of what happened earlier. "Yeah, I know." Austin said. "Hey Austin. I'm sorry about these funny vibes we have. I try to avoid them." Looking at his watch, he said, "Yeah, me too. It's getting late for me to be out at this bar with all this shit on my mind. I don't want to drink my bar away. I just needed to get some air." "You want me to walk with you?" Cynthia asked. "No thank you, I just need some time to myself, I'll see you around Cynthia." He stood up. "Yeah, around I guess." Cynthia replied as she watched Austin walk out of the bar. Austin got into his car and headed home. He decided he would take the scenic route. He hopped on the highway. While riding, he thought he had passed a car that looked just like Jasmine's. He remembered her screaming out, "Daddy, you don't love me anymore." His eyes started to tear up. Wiping his face, he turned on to his exit. He went down a street when he remembered the time two guys tried to jump him. It just so happened that Thomas was riding by. He hopped out and fought side by side with Austin as they threw a beat down on the other men. "The good times." Austin thought to himself. But then a harsh taste of disrespect came pouring in his month. When he thought about how Thomas disrespected him, the good times vanished from his mind. Before he knew it, he was pulling up at home. Those multiple shots kicked in as Austin stumbled a little, getting out of the car. He made his way into his house, after struggling to get the key in the door. He slammed the door, waking up Vicky. She got out of bed and walked into the kitchen. "Oh lord, you're drunk." Vicky said, as Austin searched in the fridge for a cool beer. "I'm not drunk. I'm just a little of tipsy." Austin said trying not to show how much he was passed his limit. "Oh yes you are." Vicky said with a smile on her face. "Honey, I'm going to go get you some clothes to sleep in." "Yeah, yeah, yeah. You do that." He said fanning Vicky away with his hand. He opened his beer and chugged it down in seconds. Still stumbling, he went to sit in his recliner. In no time, Austin passed out. The next morning came faster than Austin wanted. He woke up to the smell of fresh coffee. Getting out his recliner, he walked in to the kitchen and poured himself a cup of coffee. "I thought you would have been up sooner." Vicky said, half way dressed. "You're up and dressed early." He said. "Yes baby. I have a lot of things to do and I want to get them done. I also don't want to think too much about yesterday. Have you spoken to your daughter after all that happened?" She asked. Austin went in his pocket and pulled out a key that had flowers painted on it. He threw it on the counter. Vicky looked at Austin and said, "Now I know that's not Jasmine key. Austin, you took Jasmine's key?" "Yes." "Now look at me Austin. What they did was wrong and upsetting. What they did was very wrong. But you can forgive them. You must forgive them and move on with your life. Don't do it for them but do it for yourself. Pushing your daughter out your life because of this is not right. How do you think she feels about the fact she has hurt you? And Thomas... How do you think Thomas feel now that he had to tell his best friend that he was having sex with his daughter? Baby

104

you have to forgive them. Maybe not right away, but soon. And please check on that boy Patrick, but don't tell him about Thomas. You know that boy got a bad past and Thomas will end up missing. Then you will be mad at Patrick." Austin looked at Vicky and asked, "Are you done? Do you think they cared about how I was feeling when they were fucking? Nah, better yet. Do you think Thomas gave a shit when he was touching and fucking my daughter? Nor when he was getting our daughter, his god-daughter, pregnant? How can you want me to up and forgive them so easily? You want me to forgive them as if it was something simple, like drinking my last beer. You know what? There's something I'll have to work on." Austin said to Vicky as he stormed down the hallway. He walked into the bathroom and sat on the edge of the bath tub. Taking a moment, he reminded himself that he wasn't mad at Vicky. As he left the bathroom to go apologize, he heard the front door close. So instead, he hopped in the shower, got dressed, and made his way to his car. He tried hard to clear his mind. He put on some old school jams and vibe to the music. Shortly after, he pulled up at work, singing and feeling better about the day. "Good morning. Good morning." Austin said as he made his way into his office. "It's a new day and nothing can bring me down." he said to himself. Entering into his office, Austin scrambled through his paper work. Getting things in order and making phone calls to clients. Looking at his calendar, he seen that he was expected to call one of his loyal clients and longtime friend, Mr. Palms. So he did. "Top of the morning Mr. Palms. Just wanted to touch bases with you and wanted to know if our contract was still a go." "Well, good morning Mr. Roberts. Yes, we are.

But under one condition." "Yes, Mr. palms. What is it?" "We will have to push it back at least six months. Now I know that is asking a lot of you, but my wife is still going threw it from the death of our daughter." "Oh my God. I'm sorry to hear that Mr. Palms. I wouldn't have called with business had I known." "No, it's fine. It's fine Austin. You know that death is a painful thing to take on. But the worst thing is that before my daughter died, her and my wife were at each other throats over a sweater. A damn sweater. My wife told her to go get her own sweater and my daughter stormed out the house. After coming from the mall, my daughter sent my wife a text of the same sweater. The text read, "I guess I was forced to go get my own." Three minutes later, a truck ran a red light and hit my daughter. It killed her on impact." Mr. Palms started to choke up. "Austin, do good by your daughter because you never know when you might not see her again. I'll see you in six months. I'll call you if we want anything earlier." "Yeah, sure. And sorry again for your loss Mr. Palms." They hung up the phone and he laid back in his chair. He called Vicky's cell, but she didn't answer. He called her office a few times, but still no answer. So he grabbed his keys and headed down to Vicky's office. Austin walked to the front desk. The receptionist gave a warm greeting as she knew who he was. "Hey, I'm looking for my wife. Have you seen her?" "Yes, she told me she was going to be on site for the first few hours or so." The lady said. "Yeah, she did tell me she was going to be busy today." Austin said. "Oh, well have her call me right away." Said Austin as he left the building. Arriving at the stairs, he heard someone ask, "See you around came fast huh, Austin?" He looked back and saw it was Cynthia smiling. "Oh hey. I guess so." Austin replied nervously. "What are you doing here?" Cynthia asked. "I was here trying to see my wife, but she's not here." He answered. "Really? What floor is she on? I might know her." She's works on the fifty-seventh floor." "On the fifty-seventh floor?" Cynthia asked curiously, trying to make sure she heard Austin right." "Yeah. The fifty-seventh floor. She's a big deal around here. Victoria Roberts. Do you know her?" Cynthia froze as she knew the horrible truth about Vicky. "Oh no. I don't know her. I'm on a different floor." Cutting the conversation short Cynthia said, "I'm running extremely behind. I have to go." She rushed off. Cynthia got to the front desk to check for any messages and looked over her shoulder as Austin walked away. "He's a fine one huh?" The lady at the front desk asked. She continued, "Girl, Victoria is lucky that man loves her. Did you see those flowers the other day?" Still looking at Austin as his image faded away. Cynthia said. "Yeah, she's lucky. The flowers were nice." Then Cynthia asked. "Where's Victoria now?" "She said you two were going to be on site for a few hours." Covering for Vicky, Cynthia said, "Yeah, that's right. I thought she'd be back already to go over the rest of the paperwork. She must have made a stop on the way here. I'll be in my office if you need me." Said Cynthia, as she headed to her office. She couldn't stop thinking about Austin. "I can't believe Victoria would do that to a man like Austin." Cynthia mumbled to herself. "Do she know how much that man loves her?" Juggling her thoughts, Cynthia debated whether or not she should tell Austin. That caused her to think about her livelihood and how she needed this job. She was confused. Leave a new friend alone or make a new enemy. Either way, she knew that this situation was not going to end well. Meanwhile, Austin was still trying to figure out what he would say to his daughter and how important it was for him to forgive her. He called Jasmine, but he did not get an answer from her either. Moments later, a number that he did not recognize called in. Curious, Austin picked up. "Daddy." Jasmine said, with a cracked voice. "Jasmine, what's wrong? Whose number is this?" "I'm in the hospital. I've been trying to reach mom but she never answered. I thought you didn't want to talk to me." "Forget all of that Jasmine. Why are you in the hospital? What happened? Are you ok?" He asked nervously as his voice trembled. "It was so much blood daddy. It was so much blood." Jasmine said as she started crying on the phone. "What? Tell me baby, what happened?" "I woke up early this morning and my stomach was hurting. I went to the bathroom and blood came rushing out from under my skirt. It was all over the toilet and I fell because it was all over the floor. Daddy, the baby is gone." She said in tears. Hurting for his daughter, Austin asked, "What hospital are you at?" "CJW." "Ok, I'll be there soon." He rerouted his car and rushed to his daughter. He called Vicky again but she still wasn't answering. Arriving at the hospital, Austin rushed to the front desk. "Excuse me. I'm looking for my daughter, Jasmine Roberts. She came here earlier this morning." "Yes, she's in the women health center. Are you looking for the man that came in with her too?" The front desk asked. "It was a man with her?" "Yes. After the first ambulance came in, we had to send another one out." "No ma'am, I'm only concerned for my daughter, that's it." "Ok sweetheart. Go straight up, turn left and

108

you will see the elevator to your right. She's on the fourth floor. Austin followed the directions which lead him to another desk. "Hey, I'm looking for Jasmine Roberts. I'm her father." Austin said as he pulled his I.D out. "Yes, room four thirty-four." The nurse pointed down the hall. Austin rushed to her room. Jasmine looked up as he walked in the door. "Daddy!" She shouted. Austin rushed in and hugged Jasmine. "I thought you were in danger. I love you baby girl. Everything is going to be alright, daddy's here." Jasmine just cried as she held on tight to her father. Releasing her, Austin said, "Have you spoken to your mom?" "No, I'd thought you would have been in contact with her by now." Jasmine said. A nurse entered the room. "Hello. I am sorry again for your loss. Once the doctor runs some more tests, you can go home. I think you're doing well, so you should be out soon." The nurse explained. "That's great news Jas." Austin said. Jasmine asked the nurse, "What about the guy who came in with me?" The nurse glimpsed down at the floor and said, "I can't say. Sorry, it's not my place, but the doctor is right outside. He could possibly tell you something. I'll go get him." The nurse left the room. Austin asked, "What's going on?" Jasmine said, "I had to stay at Thomas' house because I had nowhere to go. Thomas heard me in the bathroom and called 911. Moments after the ambulance arrived, Thomas passed out." Austin thought to himself, it must have been the fight he had with Thomas. He prayed to himself that nothing major happened. "Hello. I'm Doctor Sanders. You came in with a Mr. Thomas?" "Yes, yes I did." Jasmine replied. "What's wrong doctor?" Austin asked nervously. The doctor informed them that Thomas had a small lump, about the size of a quarter in his chest near his heart. "The excitement of what happen to Jasmine shifted the lump in his chest, causing it to slightly press on his heart. But you guys saved each other if you think about it. If you were home alone, who knows how much blood you could have lost. Looking at your record, another pint or two and you might have died from blood loss. And at the same time, you were the reason Thomas' lump shifted. Over the next few months he could have died in his sleep, in his car, or just looking at television. He wouldn't have even known it was there. We still have to get the lump out and it's going to be extremely risky." Austin was relieved that the fight was not the reason Thomas passed out. Jasmine asked, "What room is he in?" "He's on the second floor. Room two twenty-eight." The doctor said as he walked out. Right away Jasmine said, "Daddy, you have to go see him." "I don't have to do anything." Austin answered as the nurse peeked her head in the room. "You will be getting released in the next forty-five minutes to an hour sweetheart." Jasmine said, "Daddy, you hear that? Forty-five minutes to an hour. You can go see Thomas for at least ten minutes. Maybe even less. He saved me daddy. And who knows what is going to happen once the doctors do surgery." Austin put his anger and pride to the side as he thought about Mr. Palms. "Ten minutes." Austin said to Jasmine as he walked out of the room. Austin headed down to the second floor. Thomas seen Austin walking in and his as heart monitor started to race. "Calm your ass down Thomas before you kill yourself. I'm not here to hurt you." Thomas just stared at Austin, waiting for him to speak again. Austin made his way around the bed and sat on a nearby chair. Thomas continued to stare at

Austin, while Austin looked at the television trying to think of something to say. "I'm sorry." Thomas said as he teared up. Austin looked at Thomas. "That doesn't make it right." Austin sat back in the chair and said, "Destiny Harper." Thomas looked at Austin and asked, "What?" "Destiny Harper. You remember her. She was so pretty and I just knew I had a chance. She was nice. I mean just my type. But man Thomas, you were head over hills for her all through college. I mean that's all you talked about." Thomas smiled. "Yeah, I remember." Austin continued, "The crazy thing was, you met her after me. But I know that's who you told yourself you wanted to marry. That's why you never married anyone. One night, she came to our apartment looking for you. She told me she had this major crush on you and I thought that was great. She promised me not to tell you because she wanted to set up something nice and romantic for you and her. I thought, 'my boy going to have the girl of his dreams and the girl of mines too.' Three days later we planned a trip for you to go to the beach with some of our friends. That night, she came over. It was about eleven o'clock. That's when the truth came out. She had her hair done, smelling good, and had a coat on. So I asked her, 'Why do you have a coat on. Its eighty degrees outside tonight.' She pushed me in our apartment and told me that I was really her crush. She explained how everything was a set up to find out when I was going to be free and alone. As I stood there in shock, she pushed me on the couch and opened up her coat. There, in front of my eyes, I seen the most beautiful girl in the school. Right there in front me with royal blue lingerie on. I mean T, if you would have seen that silk blue hugging her nice tan skin... Man she was fine." Thomas laughed. "But you see, I stopped her and kicked her out. Thomas, I knew if I was to do that. I would have hurt my best friend. I knew you had a thing for her and I knew I could never cross that line." Thomas' eyes began to fill with tears as he knew what Austin was getting at. Austin looked at Thomas and said, "My loyalty is still here. Where did yours go?" Thomas looked at Austin and said, "Forgive me and I'll show you that it just got off track." "Someday, but not right now." Austin said as he got up and walked towards the door. He turned to Thomas and he saw the pain in his eyes. Then smiled and said, "Hey T. You needed that ass whipping. That's what your mom would have said." Thomas tears ran down his face. He knew at that moment that there was a part of Austin that forgave him. Austin headed back up to Jasmine's room. He tried to call Vicky again, but still no answer. The doctor gave Jasmine her release papers and Austin helped her to the car. Finally, after the quiet ride, they arrived home. He helped Jasmine out of his car. He took her inside of the house and sat her down on the bed. "Jasmine, I'll always love you." He said as he placed her key on her nightstand. Austin stood up and Jasmine said, "I'll always love you more." Austin realized, looking at Jasmine in her bed that he had to find a way to forgive her. Austin called his secretary to tell him to reschedule his day. Exhausted, Austin headed to the recliner and dosed off to sleep. A few hours later, Austin was awaken by Vicky coming in the door. He hopped up. "What are you doing home?" Vicky asked. "Where the hell you been and why the hell you haven't called me back." "My phone was dead. Austin, relax. Damn. You still haven't answered my question. Aren't you supposed to be at work?" "No, no I don't! Not when my daughter almost bleed to death from a miscarriage!" In shock, Vicky froze. "What? Where is she?" "She's in her room." He replied. Vicky rushed to get down the hall but Austin grabbed her arm. "Why is your lipstick smeared on your face?" "Are you really asking me this right now?" Vicky asked. Austin raised his eyebrows and said, "Well?!" Still demanding an answer from Vicky. Thinking fast, Vicky replied. "Well, if you must know, I was on site with a very nice millionaire who is extremely happy with her new investment. Yes, her. As in a female. Now if we are done, I would like to go tend to my daughter who more than likely needs her mom right now." Feeling dumb about questioning Vicky, Austin sat down. Thinking about everything that was going on, Austin grabbed his keys and left the house. As he drove around, he started thinking about what Vicky said about forgiving Thomas. He then decided to go back to the hospital and explain his feelings to Thomas. Forgiving Thomas might take awhile, but he would work on that eventually. Austin pulled up to the hospital, making his way to Thomas' room. Thomas was not in there. Austin asked the nurse, "Where did they move him." The nurse said, "Thomas went into surgery." and directed Austin to follow her to the waiting room. Before Austin could get comfortable, the doctor noticed Austin from Jasmine's room. "Hello again. I'm doctor Sanders. I was the doctor upstairs with you and your daughter. Are you the only family here for Thomas?" "Yes." Austin said. "He is the only child and his mom is in a nursing home. So how did the surgery go? Good I hope. This guy is going to owe me a list of favors." The doctor looked at Austin with a steel face. He didn't laugh at Austin's joke. "Sir, I'm sorry. Thomas didn't make it through surgery." "What?" Austin asked. "I just was here. Is this one of Thomas' dumb ass games? I don't have time for this doctor. What room did you put him in?" The doctor looked at Austin. He tried to calm Austin down as he yelled, "Thomas!" "Thomas!" Tears started to form in his eyes as he told the doctor to quit playing with him. "Go get Thomas!" Austin yelled. The doctor said, "I'm sorry, sir. I'm sorry." Then he walked out of the waiting room." Austin burst out in tears as he sat down on the waiting bench. The nurse that led Austin to the waiting walked in. She was an older lady. She sat down beside Austin and put her hands around him. "Young man, be strong. Be strong. The Lord needed him." Fumbling his word and in tears, Austin said, "I need him. I needed him. Why does God hate me? What did I do?" "Son, I don't know why he wanted your friend, but I do know he doesn't hate you. Ok baby?" Still fumbling with his words Austin said, "Yes." He cried out loud once more and in tears. "I'm ok. I'm ok." Austin told the nurse as he wiped his eyes. The nurse said, "You be strong." Then she got up and left him sitting alone. Austin sat in that same chair for two hours. The same nurse walked passed Austin again and told him, "Baby, whenever you're ready. You get up and be strong. Let the lord move your feet and believe that your dear friend is with you." Sniffing his nose and wiping his teary eyes Austin said, "Yes ma'am." He took a deep breath and walked to the old nurse, hugging her. "Thank you." "You're welcome. But being strong is in you." Austin stood up straight and walked to the hospital's exit. The sun hit his face as he slowly made his way to his car. Austin headed home, trying to think of how he was going to tell Jasmine. Austin was hurting. Finally, he pulled up to his house. He sat in the car for a few minutes, gathering his strength. Stopping at the door, he took a deep breath. From the couch, Vicky could see Austin as Jasmine laid with her head on Vicky's lap. Vicky could see in Austin's face that something was not right. He came inside the family room and sat in his recliner. Vicky asked, "What's wrong?" Jasmine looked at Austin with panic on her face. Austin started to tear up. Then Jasmine set up saying, "No daddy, no daddy. Tell me Thomas made it through surgery." Austin's tears started to fall as he shook his head no. Then he finally whispered, "Thomas is gone." Jasmine screamed out and Vicky grabbed her as tears rushed down her face. While holding Jasmine, Vicky started crying herself. She asked Austin, "Are you ok?" Austin burst into tears again rushing over to Vicky. He fell to his knee as he shook his head no. "Thomas is gone. Thomas is gone." Austin repeated. They all sat in tears as Vicky said, "Come on. We can get through this. We can get through this together." Vicky pulled Austin's face up from her legs. "Baby, we are a strong family and we are going to get through this." Austin nodded his head yes. With tears still falling, he stood up. He walked to his bedroom where he cried himself to sleep. Vicky helped Jasmine get in her bed, where she did the same thing. Vicky went back to the kitchen, poured herself a drink, and dozed off on the couch as the television watched her until the next morning.

Chapter 7.

"Ring, ring, ring." "Good morning Jasmine." Patrick said, picking up the phone. "Hey. Good morning to you. Patrick, I was hoping we could do lunch and talk in person. It's been a rough few days. Maybe you could stop by my house. I really just need a friend and a laugh." "A friend and a laugh? What do you want to talk about Jasmine? I mean, do we even have anything to discuss? You're pregnant. You wasn't even going to tell me. Or, you would've just had the baby and said it was mine. Sorry, but we don't have much to talk about. I don't want to be a part of my heart being broken any more. I gave you my all. I gave you everything I could give. I gave you all I could offer and you spat in my face. Jasmine, you left me out to dry. I bet all your friends were hanging out with you and you're boo, while I was working these long ass hours to buy you a ten-thousand dollar ring. And to think, I was going to upgrade it in a year." Jasmine stopped Patrick, "I know you're hurting. I know Patrick. Can you find it in your heart to forgive me?" "Forgive? Jasmine, how about you try and forgive that nigga who came in your life and snaked his way in our relationship. I had faith in you. But you never know with people so I just let go and let God. I freed myself, knowing that he would help me, even if it would hurt. And he did. So how is Thomas? I seen you guys lock eyes in the kitchen." Patrick said. Jasmine's voice started to crack as she said Patrick, "Thomas died yesterday in surgery." "I guess your kid is not going to have a father then, huh?" Patrick said. "How could you say that Patrick? How can you be so careless about a person's life? And to let you know, there's no father and there is no baby either because I had a miscarriage. I'm sorry I hurt you Patrick. I feel your pain." Jasmine said crying. The phone went silent as Jasmine stop to wipe her tears. "Patrick, are you still there?" "Jasmine, you don't feel my pain because our pain is different. I'm heart broken and sad for being a great man to a woman who didn't care about, nor respect me. I'm hurting for being stupid and being blinded by love. I'm hurting because I wasted my time having dinner ready for you every chance I got. For rubbing you down when you were hurting and I was tired. Let's not forget running bath water and changing your flowers in your vase every two weeks just because. The fact is, I was going to end up hurting anyway because God knew your secrets and I asked him to show me them when he was ready. God knew what you were doing and it was wrong. Now you're reaping what you sowed. It's just that simple. I will get over my pain but who knows when you will feel relief from our God. We both know he doesn't like ugly." Patrick preached. Jasmine said, "I will get through this because God knows I didn't mean for any of this to happen." "Yes, you will Jasmine. I know you will get through this. The lord is a forgiving God. But when he does forgive you, and when you will have a chance to do right, please make sure you do right." Patrick replied. Jasmine felt she had a second chance with Patrick. He continued, "We had some great times. And some bad ones and we will learn from them. I wish you the best with the next man God plans to send your way." "No, wait Patrick. I can do better. Please give me a chance to make things right." Patrick hung up the phone while trying to keep his emotions together. He almost broke down. Ripped in every direction, Jasmine laid back in her bed. Staring at the ceiling, wishing she could change things. Moments later, Vicky knocked on the door and entered Jasmine's room. "Are you ok?" Vicky asked. Sitting up on her bed, she began to cry. "I've seen better day's mom. Who knew, at almost twenty something years later, I'll be sitting in this room as hurt as I am." Vicky sat down beside Jasmine. "Hurting is sometimes the best thing for us. It helps us grow and help us learn how to be better people. To ourselves and to others in our lives. You just have to take what's happening and make the best of it. Never give up when you lose people. If it's death, a heartbreak or if it's just some distance from a close friend. Never give up. It's no point. Move forward or make what's hurting you, work for you." Vicky hugged Jasmine and made her way out of the room. She walked to her bedroom where she had seen Austin. While sitting on his side of the bed, he was looking out of the window in a daze. Austin heard Vicky walk in. "Thank you for last night baby." He said. "What you mean?" Vicky asked. "Last night, I was in a crunch and I needed your words. They woke me up today in a much better mood. I'm still hurting, but I'm in a better mood. I just wanted to say thank you." Austin stood up, walked over to Vicky and hugged her tight. Vicky said. "We will get through this." Austin released her and she headed to the bathroom to get in the shower. Vicky's phone rung before she could get in the shower. It was Vicky's best friend, Michelle. "Hello." "Vicky are you ok? How is Austin? Drew and I are torn up about Thomas' death. I know him and Austin were closer than anyone we know." "Hey girl. We are all broken up about it. You know Austin is more hurt than

119

any of us, but I'm sure he will come around. Is Drew doing well?" Vicky asked. "Yeah Vicky. He's all down about it. But he knows as we get older these things are going to start happening. I just wasn't expecting it now." Michelle said. "Well thanks for calling. I have to get myself together for work." "Ok baby. Wish you guys the best." Michelle said as she hung the phone up. Vicky finished taking off her clothes and turned on the shower. She knew she needed to cheer Austin up or just relax him. So Vicky walked into their bedroom in her towel. "Vicky?" Austin called out, opening his eyes as he was laying on the bed. Vicky didn't say anything. She just looked at Austin and smiled. She turned around to walk out of the room, looking back at Austin once more before walking into the bathroom. Austin knew what that meant. He quickly took his clothes off and followed Vicky in the bathroom. She grabbed her soap and started to rub between her breast and legs. Austin stood there staring at Vicky. Austin's mind slowly began to focus on his wife. Vicky slowly came closer to Austin, rubbing on his built body as the warm water ran down him. She begin to kiss on his chest and lick his nipple. Austin started to relax as his penis stiffened. She noticed Austin swollen penis, so she gripped the base of it and started to stroke it. She made her way down Austin's body coming to her knees. She stuck his harden muscle in her mouth. Austin sighed as Vicky slowly massaged his balls with him still in her mouth. While gasping for air, she moaned. She continued to spit and rub on Austin's penis and balls. He put his foot on the edge of the tub for more leverage as he dug deeper in Vicky's throat. Vicky stopped and slowly made her way up to Austin's body and kissed him in the mouth saying, "Please get inside me." Austin quickly turned her around and bent her over. She grabbed his penis, aligned it between the lips of her vagina and Austin eased his way inside of her. They both let out a moan as they felt their bodies become one. With each stroke, Austin got deeper. With each stroke, Vicky became wetter. "Harder!" Vicky yelled with a moan. Her pussy started to squeeze Austin dick as he threw himself in her with all his force. The tension in the shower began to build higher as their emotions took over. The water ran down their bodies as Vicky screamed out. "I love you." "I love you too." Austin replied, building more tension. He started to go faster and faster as she yelled louder. Together, they climaxed. Breathing hard as he stayed inside Vicky for another moment. "I love you." She said, feeling amazed. Pulling himself out of Vicky, he said, "I love you too." The two washed off and headed into their room. Jasmine yelled down the hallway. "You'll are nasty!" Vicky and Austin laughed. "I guess I'll get ready for work. I don't want to be dragging or walking around feeling depressed. I'd rather be at work." Austin said. "I'm going to do the same." Vicky replied. They got dressed and headed to work. As he made his way to work, he tried to call Cynthia to tell her the bad news. He did not get an answer, so he figured he would try her again later. Austin arrived at his office, still thinking about Thomas. He began to regret coming in to work. After battling with himself, he found the strength to push forward and walk through the doors. Like always, he greeted everyone and made his way to his office. He tried to stick to his normal routine as he organized papers for clients. While going through the motions, a small part of him was waiting on Thomas to text or call about something stupid. But it never came. Finding focus, Austin called a few clients. He made sure that they were happy and called around his office, checking on his employee presentations. After, he decided to call Vicky. "Hello." Victoria Roberts speaking. "Hey baby, its Austin." He said. "How are you holding up?" She asked. "I'm doing well. Trying to stay busy. Just wanted to see what you were up too. I kind of miss our lunch call conversations. We used to talk about everyone at our jobs." Vicky started laughing. "Yeah, I know right. Like the girl in your office that have the dirty wigs and always trying to flip it." Austin burst out laughing and said, "She just walked passed my office." They both laughed. "So what's new in your office?" Austin asked. "I have some new hires. A new girl is working under me now. She's pretty nice. She's a hard worker, I'll tell you that. Now that I think about it, she hasn't said a word to me today. She's normally moving around and would have called me by now. I'll have to check on her." Vicky said. "Well you go take care of that and I'll take care of you later." Austin said. "You already did." Vicky said as they both laughed before hanging up. Vicky got up and walked to Cynthia's office. "Hello sweet thang." Vicky greeted Cynthia. Leaning back in her chair, Cynthia smiled and said hi. "Are you ok?" Vicky asked. "Yes, yes. How are you doing?" "Well, to be honest, my husband lost his best friend yesterday." "Oh no!" Cynthia said. "Yes, and he's all torn up about it. I see he's trying to be strong, but Thomas was his closest friend." Right away, Cynthia figured that was the reason Austin called her. Cynthia started to tear up in front of Vicky. "What's wrong? Why are you teary eyed?" Vicky grabbed a tissue and handed it to Cynthia. "Oh, nothing." Cynthia said as she took the tissue, trying to think of something to say. Cynthia just covered her month, as Vicky patiently waited on a response. Thinking fast, Cynthia said, "My cousin recently passed away back in Miami, those feelings just came back." Vicky felt bad and started to rub Cynthia's back. Going through her emotions, Cynthia just thought about the loss of Thomas and how hurt Austin must be. "I hope everything gets better for you." Vicky said as she started walking out of Cynthia's office. "Thanks, and I hope your husband feels better too." Looking at her phone, Cynthia thought about telling Austin everything. She also knew that it would make matters worse for him, so she left that idea alone. Later in the day, she thought of Austin again. In that very moment, she received a text. It was Austin. "Can you meet me at the bar today. I really need someone to talk to." Cynthia did not reply. She did not know what to say. She knew that things would get deeper between them and she did not want to be the bowling ball that wrecked the pens. A few days passed. Word spread that Thomas' funeral would be Friday. His family traveled into town. Some were invited to stay with Austin. It was not one of Vicky's favorite ideas, but she knew it was for a good reason. Austin continued to reach out to Cynthia, but she never answered nor replied to his texts. He decided it was for the best, since he is a married man. Soon, it was Friday morning. Austin woke up and looked at Vicky. He appeared to have the most focused face that she had ever seen. He got out of the bed, holding back his emotions as he went to wake everyone up. Everyone could tell that Austin was bothered and just trying to play tough. He came back into the bedroom to get his towel. Vicky said, "Austin, stop fighting it and embrace it." Austin looked at Vicky. "I don't know what you're talking about" as he made his way to the bathroom. Vicky went to check if Jasmine was up and willing to help her start breakfast. Vicky opened the door, but did not see Jasmine. "She's outside." One of Thomas' cousin said. Vicky went to the front door and seen Jasmine on the porch. "Well, it's a nice morning." Jasmine smirked. "Yeah, too bad it's a funeral today." Vicky said, "You can't be like that. You have to be strong. Take life as it comes. Your dad is already acting like he's not emotional. I'm praying he doesn't break down too bad at the funeral. But Jas, be strong for me baby." "Mom, do you hate me for what Thomas and I did?" Vicky looked at Jasmine. "No, and neither does your father. If you and Thomas were truly in love, that's just what it was. Or even if you were just getting some on the side before you got married, things just unfolded in a way you couldn't control. Now get your pretty self in here and help me cook so these weird people can get out my house." Jasmine started laughing as they both headed back inside. "Breakfast will be ready in thirty minutes." Vicky announced. Austin got out of the shower and took his time to gather his thoughts. He thought about Thomas and started to silently break down. He grabbed a pillow and covered his face as he balled into tears. He slowly calmed down, taking the pillow off of his face to make sure no one heard him. Austin dozed off for a few minutes. Vicky woke him up to let him know that breakfast was ready. Shortly after everyone ate, the limos arrived to pick them up. Family and friends followed as the limos made their way to the church. "Are you ready?"

Vicky asked Austin. He nodded his head yes. They rode in silence until they arrived at the church. Thomas' mom started crying as reality set in. Austin helped her out of the limo. They slowly walked to the church where he noticed there were fields of cars. Austin recognized good college friends, some of Thomas' old flings, new flings, and flings that just wanted to make sure that he was gone. It was amazing to see how many people showed up to give their respect. Finally, everyone was seated. The pastor led the service and reminded everyone to hold on to the good memories. The choir sang his favorite songs and a few people spoke about their crazy times with Thomas. It was time to lift Thomas' casket but they needed one more pallbearer. "I'll do it." Austin said as he grabbed his best friend's casket. The six men walked out holding Thomas. Austin looked out of the corner of his eye and seen someone that he thought was Cynthia. Paying it no mind, he continued to walk as he gently cried. They arrived at the cemetery. Austin and the other men grabbed Thomas' casket for the last time before placing it on the reels. Turning to his seat, Austin confirmed that the women was in fact Cynthia. They made eye contact, but it was broken as Austin sat beside Vicky. The pastor said his final words as the time came to lower Thomas into the ground. As the pastor prayed his last prayer, Thomas's family placed roses on his casket. Some barely made it to the casket without breaking down into tears. Austin looked back at Cynthia and they made eye contact once more. She then turned away and walked off. As the funeral was brought to a close, everyone walked to their cars to head to the repass. Austin got in the car with Jasmine. She was all cried out.

"There's something else bothering you Jas, I can tell." Austin said. "It's nothing daddy." Austin looked at Jasmine. "You thought Patrick was going to come." Jasmine nodded. Austin continued, "I knew he wasn't going to come. He have damn good reasons not to. Don't get it twisted. He's somewhere hurting for Thomas because before you and Thomas did what y'all did, it was respect between them. I know. So let's just get some food and get this day over with." When they arrived to the repass, Andrew walked up to Austin. "Hey man. How you holding up?" Andrew asked. "Ok man. Thanks Drew. I appreciate you. Where you been anyway? I haven't seen you around." Austin asked, making small talk. "Well, I've been working. Just trying to keep everyone happy." "I heard that." Austin said. They all gathered and the pastor blessed the food. Vicky walked up to Austin. "You haven't been the same since we left the cemetery. Are you ok?" She asked. "Yeah, just thinking about a lot of stuff and you know I don't like being around all these people when I have a lot on my mind. I might just head to the bar." "Ok, well just let me know. And just a heads up, I called some people and let them know we're having a little get together tomorrow night." She said, knowing he just wanted to be alone. Austin looked at Vicky with frustration, but had no energy to argue. He just said okay and snuck out of the repass. Austin arrived at his bar and made himself comfortable on a bar stool. "Hey Joe." Austin said. "What going on Austin? You just missed baby girl." "Who are you talking about Joe?" Austin asked. "The pretty thing that comes in the bar now. The girl that had you running out the door with your tale tucked between your legs." "Cynthia?" Austin asked. "Yeah, that's her name. She's been coming in the bar having one or two drinks, then runs for the door. And trust me, she's a man magnet. Everyone who comes in here tries their hand and she declines them all. I think she's gay. If she's not, she only has the eyes for one man. And that might be you." Joe said while laughing. "How long ago did she leave Joe?" Austin asked. "Hell. I'm surprise you didn't open the door for her. She just left out." Austin text Cynthia, "I'm at the bar, Joe said you just left." But she never replied. Hours passed as Austin got drunk, laughed and talked to Joe about Thomas. Austin checked his phone for the time. He noticed that it was almost ten p.m. and he had missed Vicky calls. "I'm out of here Joe." Austin said. "Can you make it?" Joe asked. "Yeah, yeah, man. I'm good." Austin yelled out. He got into his car and turned his old school jams up loud. He swerved all the way home. When he pulled into his driveway, he texted Cynthia. "I don't know why your ass is avoiding me. Especially right now." Austin stepped out of the car, falling to the ground. He laughed to himself while singing his tunes. He got up and headed to the door. Before he could get his key out, Vicky opened the door. "Get in here boy. Everyone and their momma can hear your bad singing." She said. Austin walked in the house laughing. "Vicky, don't act like you don't love my singing girl." Vicky just ignored him as he trailed her into their bedroom. Austin started taking his clothes off, leaving them everywhere as he made his way to the bed. Drunkenly he said, "Good night Vicky." and hit the bed like a sack of bricks. The next day, Austin slightly opened an eye as his head was aching. Hung over, Austin set up on his bed and seen that the time was two fourteen, p.m. "Oh shit!" He said, as he hopped up, falling over his clothes that were thrown everywhere. Vicky walked in laughing. "What's going on in here?" She asked. "Baby, I'm going to hop in the shower, can you put me some clothes out? I'm late to work." Vicky laughed even more and said, "Baby, it's Saturday. You are off today." "Oh my God." He said as he put his face in his hands. "I can't believe I was that drunk." "Yeah, you was singing and yelling last night." Vicky said as she walked over to him. "Here baby. Get up and drink this coffee. I figured I'd let you sleep in with all this stuff going on. You needed the rest." "Hey, we aren't having all those people here today, right?" Vicky smiled and said, "Yes we are Austin, so you might want to get un-hung over." "Shit! I really don't feel up for these people today. All of them going to ask me the same thing in different ways. 'How you doing? Are you ok?' I don't want to deal with them." He explained. "Well, they are friends, family and some good people from work. They all are just coming to help and support. Austin, baby? Have some drinks, laugh and have some fun. Everything we do today is to make things better." Vicky said. "I'll try." Austin said as he got up from the floor. "So, what time are they supposed to be coming?" Austin asked. Vicky smiled. "Anytime now." Austin looked at Vicky with a blank face. "What the hell you mean anytime now?" Before Vicky could say anything, the doorbell sounded. "I guess 'anytime,' just turned into right now." Vicky said as she walked out of the room. Austin struggled to get himself together. He finally made it into the shower. He finished up and made his way to the bedroom. He took his time before getting dressed, as he was in no rush to greet his company. Austin noticed that Vicky's phone kept going off so he went to check. The number had no name. When the phone stopped ringing, it had four missed calls. Austin wondered who it could be. Knowing that Vicky was off, he figured he should call it back. Austin picked up the phone as Vicky walked into the room. "What are you doing?" She asked. "Oh, your phone was ringing and I thought I'd bring it to you." He said. "In your towel?" She asked. "It was ringing and I walked over to see who it was. And I was going to put some clothes on and bring you the phone after. Why you making this a big deal Vicky?" "I'm not." She said as she started to laugh. "You just got caught snooping around being nosey, that's all." "Yeah, whatever." Austin said. "I was just curious because it kept ringing, so I looked to see who it was." Vicky grabbed the phone from Austin. The text message alert sounded. "It's the same number right?" Austin asked. Vicky smiled and said, "Yeah, it is." "I wonder who could be blowing you up like that." Vicky turned the phone around. The message was from one of Vicky's workers. They were on the block and did not know what house to go to. Vicky started laughing as she walked out of the room and called the number back. Austin got dress and made his way through the house, speaking to everyone along the way. He saw Vicky and walked up to her. "You know what baby? This is exactly what I needed." He leaned over and kissed her on the lips and said, "Thanks." "I told you baby. Great vibes heals the soul. Here's to more great vibes. Chelle! Andrew!" Vicky yelled as they walked into the house. "Hey!" They both spoke as Michelle hugged Vicky and Austin gave Andrew a hand shake. "What up good people?" Andrew asked. "Nothing much, about to holla at the fellas." Austin said. "Let's go check on them fools and see what's new." Andrew said as him and Austin walked over to the huddle of men. "Yo, Yo." Brad said. "I thought my wife fired you?" Austin asked joking. "Now Austin, if your wife fired me you'd be shit up the creek. She would come home yelling at you and taking all the madness and shit she's dealing with at work, out on you." The men laughed. "I guess you're right. I'll make sure she never fires you." The men laughed again as Corey, (another guy who worked for Vicky) said, "I hope that Ms. Heights comes here. I'll be sure to put my bid in." "Man, who you telling. I'm going to make sure, I make my move. I already think she like me anyway." Brad said. "Who is Ms. Heights?" Andrew asked. "A new hire. She been here for a few weeks now. She works right under Vicky." "Right under Vicky?" Andrew asked. "I thought some guy was working under Vicky?" "No, he got fired. Not sure what for. Not in my pay grade as they say at the office." Brad said slightly laughing. Austin said. "Now, back to this Ms. Heights. I think I spoke to her on the phone. She sounded pretty cool to me." Andrew laughed and said, "Fellas, that's what us, married men call sexy women... cool." They started laughing as Austin said, "I'm going to grab me a drink." He made his way inside of the house, grabbed a bottle of scotch and took a shot. Austin was missing Thomas as he started to tear up. Andrew walked in and saw Austin tearing up. "Hey man. Are you ok?" He asked. "Yeah Drew, I'm fine. I just was thinking how crazy and wild T would be acting right now. I mean, I know we just put him in the ground man..." Andrew leaned over and gave him a friendly hug. "Come on. You are a strong man. Everything is going to work out and get better. Go to the bathroom and clean yourself up. I'll go back and tell the guys you had to shit." "Thanks." Austin said. Then he wiped his tears and headed to the bathroom. While Austin was in the bathroom the doorbell rung. Michelle answered it saying, "Hi, I'm Michelle, Victoria's best friend." Getting himself together, Austin walked out of the bathroom back to the cookout. "Did you see her?" Brad asked. "See who?" Austin asked. "Ms. Heights." Andrew walked up to Brad and asked, "What's her first name?" Then Brad said, "Ask her yourself." While signaling that Ms. Heights was walking up. Andrew and Austin turned around and Cynthia was standing right in front of them both. "Austin right?" She asked while sticking her hand out for a hand shake." Andrew quickly said, "Hey, I'm..." But before Andrew could say anything, Cynthia cut him off. "We've met before. You're Mr. Smith." Cynthia looked at Austin, then turned back to Andrew. "How are you Mr. Smith?" Andrew looked nervous as he said. "My name is not Mr. Smith. It's Andrew." "Oh, Andrew Smith. I never got your full name." Cynthia said. "I'm sorry. Do we know each other?" Andrew asked. "Oh, I must have you confused with someone else." She said. "But I believe I have met Austin before, awhile back. Do you remember me telling you about that great movie at a bar?" Cynthia asked. While catching on to what Cynthia was saying, Vicky was walking over. It was all coming together for Austin. "Hello everyone. How is everything?" Vicky asked as she walked up. "I'm sorry, I have to go." Cynthia said. While looking Austin in his eyes, she walked off. Austin looked down at the ground and said, "Andrew, I've asked you this before. And just know that if Thomas was here, he would have beaten your motherfucking ass." Vicky looked at Austin

131

in fear, not sure of what just happened. "Man Austin, What are you talking about?" Andrew asked. Looking up from the ground, Austin looked at Andrew. Over the music you could hear him yelled. "Motherfucker are you fucking my wife?" Someone turned the music down and Michelle started to walk over. "What did he just say?" She asked. Austin looked at Vicky. Noticing her body trembling and eyes tearing up, she shook her head and said, "No, baby." At that point, Austin knew that he was getting played by his wife and his dear friend. Austin started to walk off but his feet pulled his body back as he filled up with rage. Austin turned around to head for Andrew. Andrew stood there with a nervous look on his face. Vicky was shaking from her hips down in fear. "No Austin, Stop!" Austin approached Andrew, grabbed him by his shirt and head butted him, breaking his nose on impact. Still holding on to Andrew's shirt with his left hand, Austin threw a clean right hook to Andrew's left cheek bone. As he screamed out, "Fuck you! You piece of shit!" Vicky tried to calm Austin down from a short distance, but that went wrong. He turned his attention to her, releasing Andrew. He walked up and grabbed Vicky by her throat with both of his hands. He started to squeeze while yelling, "You fucking bitch! Did you think you were going to get away with this shit?" The crowd rushed to stop Austin from choking Vicky. Michelle was still confused and tried to help Vicky. She kept hitting Austin, trying to break up the battle between him and Vicky. Austin released Vicky and looked at Michelle. "Why are you trying to help this bitch? She was fucking your husband!" Vicky looked at Michelle as Michelle tried to hop on Vicky. A few people grabbed her, taking her to the front of the house before anything else could happen. Austin was still the center of attention as he pulled out his knife. The most horrifying look was in his eyes as he looked at Vicky, then Andrew. "My heart is in pieces. Now which one of you are going to get yours cut into pieces?" Looking at Vicky, Austin started walking towards Andrew. One of Austin's cousins stepped in front of him and said, "Cousin, stop. If you do this today, you are going to jail for the rest of your life and this bitch is still going to be out here fucking." Austin looked his cousin in the eyes. His hands were still shaking from rage. He said, "Ok." as tears rushed down his face. His cousin grabbed him and they both made their way to the front yard. From the back yard, you could hear the tires speed off as Austin left the house.

Chapter 8

Speeding off, Austin drove with pain in his eyes. Again, he felt betrayed by someone he loved deeply. He felt more pain when he actually pictured Vicky letting Andrew touch her. Outraged, he thought that he should turn the car around and go kill them both. At least the embarrassment will have a sense of peace. Torn between right and wrong, he just drove. Austin had no place in mind to go, so he ended up at his bar. He walked in tense as he walked towards the bar. Joe said, "Hey Austin." But Austin walked right passed Joe and went behind the bar. He grabbed the bottle of Johnny Walker and started pouring it in a shot glass. One of the guys that were sitting at the bar looked at Austin. Defending Joe, he said, "You can't come in his bar like that. Who do you think you are?" Joe seen that there was something wrong with Austin. It was definitely not just a stressful day at the job. So Joe tried to get the man to back off. But before he could get a word out Austin yelled, "Motherfucker, do I know you! No, fuck that! Motherfucker, do you know me?" Austin walked towards the man sitting at the bar. With a fearless attitude Austin said, "I put my hard earned money into this bar. Me and Joe pay taxes in here. I don't see you paying shit! By the looks of it, your motherfucking ass not even spending no real money!" Then he knocked the man's beer over. The man stood up and said, "I will fuck you up man!" Austin tried to hop over the bar while yelling, "Let me see you try it, you punk motherfucker!" Joe grabbed Austin before he could get over the bar, pulling him to the back room. "Calm down!" Austin was still yelling. "Joe, he don't know! He don't know I will kill his ass!" "Calm down! Gain control of yourself Austin!" Yelled Joe. "Sit down." He said as he pulled up a chair. "Now I've been in business with you for years. I've never seen you lash out at anyone in this bar. Even if they were wrong. Now tell me what has gotten into you." Austin sat in the chair as his face swelled. Tears seeped in his eyes while he mumbled out, "Vicky cheated on me." "Come again." Joe said. "Vicky cheated me." Austin repeated. "What!? When? With who?" Joe asked. Austin dropped his head and quickly picked it up saying, "With Andrew." "With Andrew?" Joe asked as he tried to figure out who Andrew was. Then it hit him. "Oh, Michelle's Andrew?" Joe asked. "Yeah, that motherfucker." Austin said sadly. "Well listen Austin. That don't mean go around starting stuff with just anyone. Hell, that man been coming here having a beer or two and just relaxing for months now. You need to go apologize. But before you do, calm down man. Just relax and take a breather. And look, I know you a good man Austin. Don't let other people's ignorance bring you down. Vicky went out here and cheated on her husband with her best friend's husband. That just disrespectful. Sometimes bad things happen to good people so it can clear a way for good things to enter. You follow me? Now I've always been straight with you. So, like we say in the old days, 'if she freaking around she's a freak. And if she winning along with you she a winner.'" Austin said, "Spare me the details Joe." "No, I want you to hear this man. I love you like you my own Austin, so listen up. You mad at this woman and this man for doing what they did. Know that it's a good reason to be mad. It's a good reason to feel hateful and just want to snap both their necks. But if you do, that will make you just as bad as them. You have to find peace in yourself and move on. They will get their karma. And this karma is a very bad thing to play with." Austin took a deep breath. "Yeah, I guess you're right. One day I'll forgive them. But I tell you right now Joe, I don't plan on forgiving anyone and I want a divorce. Andrew might not want to cross my path any time soon." "I understand. Just do it the right way. Don't go out here fighting and acting crazy." "Well, it's a little too late for that." "What do you mean by that?" Joe asked. "Well, I found out at the cookout we had and I kind of broke his nose." "What! Are you serious?" Joe asked. "You shouldn't have done that Austin. They pulled you out of your character." "What was I supposed to do?" Austin asked with a straight face. "You found out at the cookout? Well, how did you find out?" Joe asked. "You know Cynthia? That girl that comes here." "Yeah, the pretty girl that ran you out of here the other day." Joe replied. "Yeah, her. Remember the whole Mr. and Mrs. Smith thing she told us about, with her boss? That was Vicky and Andrew." "Wow, that's bad man. I see why you went off." Joe said as he sat in a chair beside Austin. "My best advice son, is to be strong. Don't make any decisions while you're mad. Now relax for a minute and come grab a cold one with this man, before you push our business out the door." They got up and headed back to the bar. Austin stood up as he gathered his thoughts. He walked out from behind the bar and saw the man that he was arguing with. Joe made eye contact with Austin as he kept watching. Austin walked up to the guy and said, "Hey man. I want to apologize to you. I know you were just protecting Joe. He's like a father to me. I'm just having a real fuck up day man." The man looked at Austin and said. "The names Paul." "The guy pulled his pant leg up and showed Austin a peg leg. "I know all about having a fucked up day." Embarrassed, Austin sat down beside the man. "Damn man, I didn't know." Paul said, "People never notice anything when they're mad." They both chuckled. Joe poured them a drink saying, "Tonight is on your tab Austin." "Yeah, yeah I know." Throughout the night, Paul had told Austin how he was in the war, lost friends, and how he lost is leg. He also told Austin how he came home to find his wife had left him and moved on with some rich guy. Austin couldn't believe the war stories and how much this man has been through. Austin admired how he still found a way to smile and be happy. Paul told Austin that when times get real hard, he just drops down where he is and pray. He even smiles right after and says, "Thank you lord." as if he knew his prayer was already answered. They continued sharing life stories when Austin's phone went off. It was Cynthia, texting Austin. "Hey, Austin are you ok?" Austin stared at the phone, focusing on the text. Drowning out what Paul was saying, he tried to figure out what to reply. He noticed hours had passed, then realized he didn't have anywhere to go. He text back. "I'm coming over. Be there in ten minutes." Cynthia text back. "Now?" But Austin never looked at his phone, he stood up and said, "It's been great talking to you and sorry again about earlier Paul." Then Austin rushed to put on his jacket and headed out the door. While getting in his car, his phone went off. It was Vicky, Austin looked at the phone and pressed the ignore button. Then pulled off, making his way to Cynthia's house. Minutes later, he pulled up at her house. Cynthia opened the door in her gym clothes, looking amazing. "What are you doing here? Why did you come here?" Cynthia asked. "I have nowhere else to go. I can't go to my best friend's house because he's dead. I can't go home because my wife is part of the problem. I can't go to my daughter house because she cheated on her fiancé and she's not a great option to be around right now." "So get a room." Cynthia said. "Are you really going to tell me to get a room? This is unbelievable. I can't get a room because my wallet is at home. Look Cynthia I'm not going to go back and forward with you. Can you help me or not?" Austin asked. Cynthia looked at Austin and pushed the door open. Austin walked in the house. Cynthia locked the door and walked towards the living room. Austin followed her. "Make yourself at home." Cynthia said as she sat down on the couch. "I'm sorry you had to find out this way." Cynthia said, looking down as she rubbed her palms. "Yeah, sure you are." Austin said with a slight attitude. "Excuse me." Cynthia said. "I didn't mean for it to come out like that." "It just bothers me that you knew about this the whole time and didn't say anything before. I mean, how long have you known?" Austin asked. Cynthia looked at Austin and said, "I knew when I ran into you downtown at the office building." "But I asked you did you know her." Austin said. "Yes, I know, I know. I didn't know what to tell you. When I put two and two together, I didn't know what to say. I mean, what should I to do? Tell my boss' husband, who I have some kind of feelings for, that she's cheating on him. No Austin, I couldn't do that. But I knew you were a great man who didn't deserve to be getting stabbed in the back. When I found out about Thomas, she was just out

139

sleeping around. Most likely sleeping around when you were hurting from Thomas' death. I knew I had to say something. I mean, I just moved here. I've only been here a few months. How am I going to survive living here if I don't have a job?" Cynthia stood up pacing back and forward, putting her hand on her head. "Oh my God. How am I going to keep my job now, your wife!" "Ex-wife." Austin said. "You know what I mean. Anyway, Vicky is like an animal. She pulls up dirt on people and have them without a job in weeks. What am I going to do?" Cynthia asked Austin in panic. "Calm down, calm down." Austin said as he stood up to sit her back down on the couch. He looked at her and said, "You did me a favor and now it's my turn to help you. If Vicky tries anything, I will help you." "How?" Cynthia asked still in panic. "Look, don't worry. I'll pay for your mortgage until you get straight. Now calm down." "Are you serious? You would really help me? I'm so thankful." "Yeah. I mean, who knows how long this has been going on or how long this would still be going on." He said. Cynthia looked at Austin. "My position has been empty for at least a year, you know?" "Why does that matter?" "She told me she hid it from the last guy. Catching on to possibly how long, he said. "Are you fucking kidding me? They've been doing this shit for that long?" Austin's calmness turn into anger as he began to hurt again. "I'm going to kill that bitch!" He said as he stormed toward the door. Cynthia trailed him, finally making her way in front of Austin before he could open the door. "Stop Austin. Calm down." She said. "You want me to calm down Cynthia? How can I? When this bitch was out sucking dick then coming home and kissing me! Then that motherfucker Andrew going to act like he was

140

my friend, my homie. Did you know today at the cookout, I was feeling bad about Thomas and he was there talking about 'stay strong,' like I could lean on him. But he was leaning in my wife." Austin sat down on the stairs next to the door. "I don't know what to do, I don't know. I mean, I do right. I helped this women with any and everything and this is what she does. I just don't get it." Austin said as tears began to run down his face. Cynthia stood speechless, trying her best to come up with the right words to say. Then, she blurted out, "Napoléon Hill!" "What? He was sleeping with Vicky too?" Austin asked. "No, no. 'Strength and growth only comes from continuous effort and struggle.' It's a quote he said. I heard when I was a kid. It's something I use to tell myself when I was in a bad place in my life. This pain and hurt will pass, but you must keep moving forward Austin. Now look, I can tell you've been drinking. Let me cook you some food and we can just talk and relax without all this crazy shit." Austin took a deep breath, stood up and walked towards the kitchen. He looked back as Cynthia was turning on the alarm. "What's all that for?" Austin asked. "Just in case you're crazy ass try to leave and do some T.V snapped shit. I'll know to call the cops." They both laughed and made their way to the kitchen. "So, what are you going to cook for a heartbroken, depressed, lonely man?" "Well, I figured I'd cook you some steak, potatoes, rice, and maybe a warm piece of bread. Oh, and give you a cold beer to go with it." "Damn Cynthia you know how to make a man feel better." Austin said. "Well, I'm glad I can make you feel good for a moment. I'm damn sure not cooking your black ass that tonight. I have some leftovers from last night. Meatloaf and mash potatoes." Cynthia said smiling. "That was fucked up." Austin said as Cynthia chuckled. "I thought you were going to hook me up." "I did. I'm letting you stay here. Plus, you looked like you needed a laugh." "Yeah, I hear you, thanks" Austin said. "I'm going to take me a shower. I just came from a run." "So you're not even going to make my plate?" Austin asked. "Umm, no. It's easy to find things. And I know I told you to make yourself at home." Cynthia said as she walked out smiling. "Don't burn my house down with the microwave." She yelled. "Whatever!" Austin replied. On his phone, he noticed Vicky's 24 missed calls and 17 voicemails. Frustrated, he turned his phone off and went to the fridge to grab the leftovers. As he ate he thought about what Joe had told him. He finished and began washing the dishes when he heard the shower turn off. Austin made his way to the living room to sit in silence. "Well, isn't this cheerful." Cynthia said as she walked in the living room smelling like dove. She was dressed in boy shorts and a big T-shirt on. "What?" Austin asked slightly checking Cynthia out. "Come on Austin. You're sitting in here alone, looking like a sad animal. I know this just happened, but I don't want you sitting around sulking. Get up and go take a shower. You need to wash all that sad and madness off you because it smells bad." Austin said. "Just be easy with me, damn. I'm all pissed off and don't know who to take it out on." Cynthia got serious and said, "I get it Austin. I really do. But you have to take control of what's going on. It's going to be hard but just try and focus on relaxing and having a clear mind. Not thinking about all that craziness. I'm sure you're going to have plenty of time for that. So for now, just relax and go get in the shower. I have something nice in mind that I think would cheer you up when you get out." "Where is your bathroom?" Austin asked. "On the other side of the kitchen, near the guest room. Oh wait, that one isn't fix yet. I'm redoing the bathroom in there. You'll have to go upstairs to my room to use the shower. You have to excuse the door being off. I'm getting a new door for that bathroom soon." Cynthia said as she smiled. "Ok, cool. You really need to cut back on the fixing houses channel. Where am I going?" Austin asked. She laughed and answered him. "It's the third door on the right. Just keep around, you'll see the bathroom. Austin walked up the stairs checking out Cynthia's house. Noticing her fine taste in paintings and furniture. He came to the bedroom door and was very pleased with it. It look like a room out of a magazine. The room color was light gray and it had light gray and white drapes that were breaded at the headboard of the canapé. Laying over the headboard was a light that softly deemed the room. The thick white covers and silk sheets were pulled back on the side of the bed that Cynthia slept on. Impressed, Austin headed to the bathroom to a stand up glass shower that was made of gray marble with matching double sinks. Austin got in the shower, washing up and thought about Vicky. Austin started to cry in the shower. After he got himself together he stepped out the shower. He realized he didn't have towel. "Cynthia! Cynthia!" Austin called out. Moments later Cynthia came to the door. "What's up Austin? She asked. "I need a towel." "Why didn't you asked before you got in?" Cynthia asked joking. "Maybe if your ass gave me a little more hospitality, I would have remembered." "Yeah, ok." She left to get him a towel then came back into the bathroom but Austin had soap in his eyes as he stepped out of the shower. He forgot that she didn't have a door. "Here you go." She said as Austin stuck his hand out." "Oh my God!" Cynthia said. "What you can't find the towels?" He asked. "No, I don't have a door and you're naked in my bathroom." "Oh shit!" Austin said taking the towel and covering up his penis. "Just to let you know, it's cold in here if you were looking. This is not normal." Laughing and thinking about how Austin's strong and tight body looked. She thought to herself. "Damn, he look this good cold, wonder how he would look hot." She tried to take one more peak before she left out but she got caught. "What are you looking at?" Austin asked. "Oh, umm. I was just making sure you were ok. I laid some clothes out for you." She said, eyeing Austin's wet muscles. "But I see you're good, so I'm just going to go back to the living room." He wondered what kind of clothes she could have for him as he dried off. Walking out of the bathroom, he seen sweat pants and a graphic shirt that had cats on it. "What the hell." he thought to himself. But he had no clothes, so he put them on. When he walked down the stairs, Cynthia started laughing. "I didn't think you were going to put them on. I thought you were going to put your clothes back on." "I thought you were helping me. You're over here making me look like a clown." Austin said pouting. "Yeah, whatever. You have it on now so sit down. I have some wine and cards. The best game out of seven wins." "Cynthia, I don't feel like playing no damn cards." Cynthia looked at Austin. "Look dude, sit down and take a chill pill. You're blowing my vibe." Austin frowned his face up and sat down on the floor beside Cynthia. "First, I'll make us something to drink. Then let me beat that ass in cards." "The only games I knew how to play are deuces and tunk." Austin told her. "Tunk it is. Pour your own poison." Cynthia said. The two sat down and ended up playing eleven games while drinking two bottles of wine. "I haven't play cards like that since Jasmine was seventeen. We would play for quarters. Those were the good times." Austin said, looking at Cynthia. He signed and said, "To be honest, I think that when Jasmine was about to turn eighteen, that was the first time I caught Vicky cheating on me." "Wait, this is not the first time this happened?" "Sorry to say it, but nope. It sure isn't. Billy Johnson Jr. The man swore up and down he didn't know about me. He said that Vicky told him that we were broken up. I started to beat his ass. But then I thought, "what if she did tell him that." "How did you find out?" Cynthia asked. "I pulled up to a red light with Jasmine in the car. I believe I would have done the unimaginable if Jas wasn't in the car with me that day. But I followed them and he stopped the car. Then all of a sudden she stepped out. Before I could do anything, he had left. I wasn't going to speed behind him with my daughter with me. So I pulled off. Jas said, "Daddy, no one is perfect. I looked at her and she said, "Promise me you will work it out." "I did. At least I thought I did. The worst part about it, is knowing that you give someone all of you and that's not good enough for that person you loved." Cynthia looked at Austin and said, "You're good enough for me." Austin sat speechless, not knowing how to reply back. The two of them sat there staring at each other. Austin leaned over to kiss Cynthia's soft lips. He connected as she kissed back. She gently grabbed his face. Still kissing, Austin started to make his way over to

Cynthia. He started to rub her body and pull her closer to him. They were drunk off each other's affectionate kiss that held a sweet wine taste. Austin unlocked from Cynthia lips and started to kiss her neck as she gasped for air. Moaning to the sensational feeling Austin was applying, Austin released Cynthia's neck. Just for a slight second, taking his shirt off. Amazed at Austin's fit body, Cynthia grabbed him closer as she rolled on the floor. On top of her, Austin put his hand under her shirt. He felt no bra. Feeling her hard nipples, he lifted her shirt and started to put her nipples into his mouth. Cynthia closed her eyes as she moaned out once more in passion. She lowered her hand, searching for Austin's shaft. While indulging on Cynthia's breast, Austin's half way aroused penis went full throttle. Cynthia finally made contact with Austin's thick, long penis as it poked out of the sweatpants. Cynthia gripped Austin's penis and slightly stroked it as she began to get wet. So wet, that her pajama pants were getting damp between her legs. Pulling Cynthia's pants down, Austin kissed her gently on her shoulders. Looking for her vagina, Austin removed Cynthia's hand from his penis. She threw her hands back while relaxing, drunk off of Austin's passion. Austin found the jack pot. The route to Cynthia's soul. Austin lined himself up, grazing her vagina lips as his tip got wet. He could feel the heat and warmth from Cynthia's inside. Austin angled himself to push inside of Cynthia when suddenly, Cynthia's hands stopped him. She scooted away from him, pulling her pants up. Taking deep breaths, Cynthia said, "Wait, wait Austin." Pulling herself away from his arms while fixing her shirt. "We don't need to be doing this. We are not supposed to be doing this."

Shaking her head. Lost, confused, and horny Cynthia was trying to come up with a reason why not. Austin looked at Cynthia saying, "This is what we want. This is what we both want. You have major feelings for me and I have them for you. I don't understand why we shouldn't." Cynthia stood up off the floor and looked down at Austin. "Your wife is somewhere embarrassed. Crying her eyes out and sad as fuck. And we're in here doing this. I don't know if I can go through with this. I don't know what to think right now." Cynthia said. "Do you hear yourself?" Austin asked Cynthia. "We never would have had a chance, but we do now. I'm done with my wife. I'm done with getting cheated on. I'm done with not being loved right. Giving my all and her just giving some. I can't deal with it. And you know we should try and make this an us." Pacing back and forward Cynthia said, "No, no, no. This is not right Austin. You are mad right now. You are upset. I'm trying to make you feel better. What is going to happen to me weeks from now? You are going to forgive Victoria and I'm going to be here head over hills for a married man. First, this road is extremely dangerous. How do I look, rushing into a relationship for you. Not with you, because this is just about you." Austin cut her off, grabbing her hands saying, "This is not for me. We can go slow. Figure things out. I mean, you just don't have to say no to me. I'm getting a divorce. It will just take some time. And that's what we can do until then, just take our time." Cynthia looked at Austin. "Look, tell me something Austin. How long do you think it going to take her to cheat again?" Austin said, "I know she's not because she knows she fucked up. This is my drawing point and she knows that. She would try and do anything

147

to make me see she would change." Cynthia said, "Exactly. And when she does prove to you that she's not going to cheat again, you are going to go back and enjoy your happy life and I'm not getting involved." Cynthia pulled her hands back with force saying, "I'm not doing this again." "Wait, what you mean again?" Austin asked. Cynthia ignored the question and said, "Austin. As you can see, I have laid out covers for you. I hope you sleep well. I'm going to my room. I found a church nearby. I'll be there on time. I expect you to be gone when I get back. Lock the door on your way out." Austin looked at Cynthia speechless, wondering how a great moment went so bad so fast. Cynthia turned and walked out. Austin sat down on the couch, lost and confused. With his mind racing, Austin laid back searching for a peace of mind. An hour or so past when Austin had finally fallen asleep. But not for long. He was interrupted by the slam of a door. Austin opened his eyes, noticing that it was daylight outside. He got up, looked out of the window and saw Cynthia backing out of her driveway.

Chapter 9.

Frustrated and pissed off, Austin lays back on the couch. He turned his phone on and saw Vicky left him more text messages and voicemails. All of his feelings for forgiveness were blinded by pain. He tossed his phone and sat back on the soft pillows, thinking about his last encounter with Cynthia. "I can make this work," he thought to himself while day dreaming. He was interrupted by his phone going off, it was Jasmine. Not wanting to deal with her, he ignored the call. He just needed a break from everyone. He decided to go to Thomas' gravesite to find a piece of mind. He put on his clothes and wrote a short note for Cynthia on his way out. The note read; "Hopefully I could get that steak and potatoes someday, on better terms. Hopefully we can have a chance to talk. See you around." Austin sat the note on the kitchen table where it could be seen. He grabbed his keys, and left out of the door. Before he could get to his car, he got another call from Jasmine. He still wasn't picking up. He thought that if it was a life and death situation, she'd leave a voicemail or text. Austin turned his music up and headed to visit Thomas' grave. As he rode in his car, Vicky called and left another voicemail. Frustrated, Austin turned the bluetooth on in his car and let the voicemail play. "Austin, this is me as you know. What I have done to you has embarrassed me, embarrassed our family, and most of all embarrassed what's important you. I understand that this is not the first time this has happened and I know that you are a great man." Vicky explained as she chocked up on the phone. "Baby, I truly love you. I don't know how this happened or how it even got this far. I need you to forgive me baby and come home. We can talk this out." Right then he ended the voicemail. Confused and in pain because of the disrespect, hurt, and humiliation he was force to wear. He knew that he still loved his wife in some way, but the mixed emotions for Cynthia was eating him alive. He began to believe he didn't want to be with Vicky anymore. However, he knew that Cynthia was right. After a few months or years, he would probably forgive Vicky and work on his marriage. Lost in his emotions, pain and love were pulling him into different directions. He arrived at Thomas' grave site. "Man, oh man. It's been some shit happening out here man. I mean, some serious shit. Jasmine had a miscarriage. I saw Cynthia at my bar, and it turns out, she works with Vicky. Ain't that some shit." He said laughing. "I mean, there she was, describing Vicky to me T, and I didn't think once, 'oh shit, that sounds like my wife.' Thomas, the whole time she was telling me how my wife was cheating on me." Tearing up and starting to get upset, he continued. "What am I going to do? What am I going to do man!?" He yelled. He stood up and yelled once more, "What the fuck am I going to do? You're gone. I think I love a woman I barely even know. My daughter is heartbroken. But how can I comfort her knowing she did the same thing her mom did to me!" Letting out all emotions, Austin burst into tears. As he was crying, he began to get even madder. "Yo T, Fuck that bitch! Fuck Vicky! All this time and love I put into to this marriage and this bitch gone cheat on me! She gone play

150

me like I'm some sucker! Then she told me she needed me to forgive her. No. Fuck that and that bitch! She needs to forgive her damn self. I'm not going to forgive shit!" He started to think about Vicky and Andrew. A cold breeze blew through the air. It raised goose bumps on his arms and neck. At that moment, he realized he was acting out his character and thought about Paul from the bar. He remembered how Paul said he would drop to his knees and pray when things got hard. So, that's what Austin did. "Lord, help me be strong. Help me find the right way to go." He prayed as tears continued to roll down his face. "Lord, I need your help. Guide me through these wicked woods and dark storms I am going through. This pain is too much and this weight is too heavy. Help me lord and I thank you." He opened his eyes, wiping the tears from his cheeks. Right away, his phone went off. He stood up, it was Patrick. "Mr. Roberts, my man. I need you to come over right now! It's Jasmine! She's outside my house screaming and yelling. She threw a brick through my car window and everything. I called Mrs. V, but she didn't pick up. Man, she's tripping and I'm going to get her ass locked up if you don't come!" "I'm on my way!" Austin said, running to his car and speeding off. About fifteen minutes later, Austin pulled up. Jasmine was banging on the door screaming. "I see you Kelly! You're fucking Kelly!" "Jasmine, what's going on!?" Austin yelled as he ran to her. "Daddy! He's in there with some nurse bitch from his hospital!" She yelled at the door continuing to bang on it. Seconds later the police pulled up. Walking up to Austin and Jasmine the officers asked, "Are you two the owners of this house? Austin said "No, My daughter and her boyfriend just broke up and she's mad. Sir, I just pulled up." "Ok, I understand. We had a call about some women breaking and busting windows on car. Are you her?" The officer asked Jasmine. Scared, she didn't say anything. "Ok, we have to take you down town for property damage." "What?" Jasmine asked as she started crying. "No, no, I have things in this house." She tried to explain. Austin said, "Sir, she's not a threat. I can take her home." The officer sized Austin up and said, "Back off or you are going with her." Frustrated, Austin said, "Look got dammit. This is my daughter. She is not a threat!" Then he yelled at Patrick, "Get your ass out here, now!" The officer got loud saying. "Look, she has busted the car up and damage the house door. She is going down." By that time, another officer was walking up. "She's not going anywhere!" Austin said, stepping in front of Jasmine looking the officer in his face. Patrick opened the door as he seen the tension between the officer and Austin. "Sir, I don't want to press charges. I just want her off my property." The officer said, "No, it's too late. They both are resisting arrest and then he called in for back up." "Austin, what's going on here?" A voice asked, knocking the focus off of the angered officer?" I was in the area and remembered this address." "Sergeant Taylor?" Austin asked. "Sergeant Taylor, I was trying to explain to this officer that Jasmine and Patrick are going through a tough break up and he's trying to be super cop and arrest me and Jasmine." Austin explained. "Officer Johnson, is that what's happening?" Sergeant Taylor asked." No sir. I told him that she did property damage and she had to come down to the station but he wouldn't let me arrest her." "Sergeant Taylor looked at Patrick's car and asked, "Jasmine, did you do that?" "Yes," she answered right away. "Austin, you and I have known each other for a very long time. Hell, we played cards at this very house. Trying to scare this little punk straight when he was messing up in them streets." Sergeant Taylor said. "Jas, get the car fixed and stay away from here unless Patrick approves you to come. Austin I'll see you around. Officer Johnson, go to your car and tell dispatch that everything is ok and settled." "Yes sir." The officer said with an attitude and walked away. "Jasmine, why are you over here acting crazy?" Sergeant Taylor asked. "I've never seen you act this way." Jasmine sighed, still shaken up from almost being arrested. "Patrick has another woman in there. I knew he was cheating on me." Looking at Patrick, Austin butted in and asked, "Patrick, were you cheating?" He looked at Austin and said, "Come on Mr. Roberts. You really think I'll go through asking you for your permission to marry Jas if I was cheating? As we both know, she is pissed because she messed up. Yes, I have a girl that works with me over here, but no I'm not fucking her. She was here no longer than ten minutes before Jas popped up, unannounced. She is trying to work on things that's never going to work again. Look Mr. Roberts, I understand your loyalty is to your daughter. I can definitely understand that. If I was cheating, I would have an ass whipping coming to me. But the truth is, I wasn't. She messed up a good thing." Austin understood where Patrick was coming from. He knew that Patrick loved his daughter dearly. Sergeant Taylor said, "Well, I don't know what's going on nor who did what. But we have to come to a solution on what we're doing here. Patrick, are you done with Jasmine?" Patrick looked at Jasmine and wanted to say no really bad, but he knew that one more chance was too much. "Yes!" Patrick said with his chest out. Jasmine started to tear up as she walked to Austin's car. "Jas, Jas!" Austin called out, trying to get her attention. He looked at Sergeant Taylor and said, "Thanks man, I appreciate it." Before Austin could walk off, Patrick said, "I'm sorry Mr. Roberts, I just can't right now." "I know son, just be strong." Sergeant Taylor trailed Austin as they walked towards Jasmine. "Now Jas? You have to stay away. Next time I might not be here. You also have to fix what you did." Holding back tears she nodded her head. Austin got into the car. "Thanks again Taylor. I'll tell Joe to put you on my tab for $100 on your next visit." "No problem Austin. Just take care of your baby girl." Sergeant Taylor said. "I'll come back and get your car later." Austin said to Jasmine. They rode in silence for about five minutes. Then Austin said, "Where the hell did you get a brick from Jas. I can't believe you're out here acting like this. And let me ask you something. Do you really think Patrick was cheating on you?" As they rode, Jasmine looked at Austin and said, "No." A tear came down her cheek. "So why the hell are you mad at him? I mean, what is the problem? Say for an example he was talking to or dating that girl, how do you feel it's your place to tell him that he can't date anyone else? Is that really your place?" "It's just not fair! It's not fair dad!" Jasmine blurted out and burst out in tears. Austin seen Jasmine's face and knew that she was sorry about what had happened. But he also knew that she finally realized it was over between her and Patrick. "I wanted to show him that I'm not a bad person. I wanted to let him know daddy. I just know if I had one more chance I wouldn't mess it up. I wouldn't daddy I swear. I just need Patrick to

154

know that." Austin looked at Jasmine as he came up to a red light. "Your mom said those same words to me years ago." "What are you saying daddy? Mom cheated on you again?" She asked. The light turn green and Austin ignored the question. "Look baby, you just have to face what you've done to this man. Knowing that you're wrong and he might not ever forgive you. But I do know that everything that is going on, will pass." Austin and Jasmine rode in silence for a few more minutes before arriving at home. Vicky was not there so Austin decided to go grab his wallet and maybe some clothes to sleep in. "Come on, I'm sure your mom will be home soon to help out with this situation." They both walked in the house. Jasmine went into the living room and Austin went through the kitchen straight into the bedroom. While passing through the kitchen he noticed several wine bottles in the trash can. Finally walking in the bedroom he saw there were pictures laid all across the bed with used tissues. He walked closer to the pictures. He seen that they were pictures of him and Vicky. Their wedding pictures, pictures from some of their trips and just regular pictures she took of them laying around the house. The pictures brought back memories as he picked one special picture up. It was the night that Austin proposed to Vicky. That same night, Jasmine was conceived. Austin thought about that special moment and picked up another picture. It was a picture of Vicky, Michelle, Thomas and Andrew smiling at a card game that Vicky just had to have that day. Austin thought about how much she wanted to see Andrew that night. That night, Vicky kept asking Michelle about when Andrew was going to get there. He threw the picture on the bed, grabbed his wallet and headed to the closest. Austin packed his gym bag full of clothes. He balled up his two and three thousand dollar suits without a care. He went to grab a few pairs of shoes when he saw something balled up in the corner of the closet. He grabbed the unknown piece of clothing and opened it up. It was white lingerie that was stuck together. Austin's anger was over powered by hurt. He grabbed his bag and headed to the kitchen with the lingerie still in his hand. He heard Vicky walk in while talking on the phone. "Listen mom, I messed up. How do I fix it? I love Austin. I don't know what to do mom. Help me please!" She cried to her mom. She turned around from locking the door and saw Austin standing behind her. She hung the phone up and just looked at Austin. She had no clue what to say. Then Austin said, "It's nothing." "What?" Vicky asked. "You were asking your mom, what can you do to fix us. I'm telling you, it's nothing you can do about us. We are over." He said. "Austin, baby please. We can work this out." "Oh, we can huh? Well, let's start off with you telling me the truth. How long have you been cheating?" Vicky looked choked up as she just stared at Austin. She hadn't took notice of what he had in his hand. "Baby, please!" Vicky begged. "Baby please what, Vicky?" Austin asked loudly. "You can't even look me in my face and tell me the truth." He attempted to walk out of the door. "No, stop! Stop!" Vicky yelled, getting the attention of Jasmine as she rushed over to the two fussing. "A little over two years Austin." Vicky said. Austin just stared at Vicky with a blank face. Jasmine asked, "Two years for what?" "I'm sorry." Vicky said once more as Austin just stared then said, "This is crazy, fucking crazy." "I'm sorry Austin. I

156

mean, I love you." Vicky said, rocking back and forward trying to convince Austin. "Baby we can make this work." Those words set Austin off. He rushed Vicky, grabbing her by her shoulders and pushing them flat against the door. "We can't work shit out! You fucked up! You cheated the first time and God knows it took everything I had to forgive you. I prayed and cried and prayed and cried asking the lord to give me strength. Right when I had strength... Right when I was all in...You pull this shit again!" Vicky was extremely afraid. The look in his eyes had shown that his heart was in pieces. The love that he had for her was limited. It was pouring out as hate. Tears slowly fell down her face as she was scared, regretting her foolish ways. "I am tired! I am prayed out! I do not forgive you! Victoria, I am divorcing you." Austin said calmly, but his voice was still filled with anger. Releasing Vicky from his grips, he just stared at her. Calmly he said, "Vicky, move from the door." Shaking her head she said, "No, I love you. We can make this work." "Move Vicky." She stood in front the door. "I can't let you leave, I love you. I'm sorry Austin." Frustrated, Austin grabbed Vicky by her shoulders. Pulling her with force and pushing her against the wall beside the door. "Daddy! Stop!" Jasmine said, scared for her mother's life. "I'm leaving." Releasing Vicky, he opened the door when he realized he still had the lingerie in his hand. He looked back at Vicky at said. "The sad thing is, you been fucking him unprotected." Vicky just looked at Austin. "No, don't say a word. I see all of him on here." He said as he threw the lingerie at Vicky. He grabbed his bag, looked at Jasmine and said, "I'm sorry baby girl, but no promises are going to be made this time around." Then he walked out of the door.

Vicky slid down to the floor with her back touching the wall and screamed. Jasmine rushed over to comfort her mom. "I'm sorry Jas, I really am." Meanwhile outside, Austin got into his car and pulled off. His rage started to calm and the pain of being heartbroken set in. He headed in the direction of a hotel outside of town. Getting settled in, he relaxed and tried to take a nap but he could not due to the stress. He figured he would watch a few movies and catch up on Sports center. Hours passed and the television left Austin bored. So he cleaned up, got dressed and ordered an Uber. Within minutes the Uber was at the hotel and Austin set off to his bar. He walked into the bar and noticed it was slightly packed. "Joe, What's up." Austin asked as he set down on the stool. "Austin, how are you? Are you ok? You ran out of here mighty fast the other night." Clearing his throat Austin said, "Yeah man, I'm good. I've just been stressed out lately. First Thomas, then this shit with Vicky. It's all just been a little too much. I just want to have some me time and just chill man. Fix me up something nice Joe." Austin said. "Coming right up, I have just the thing." "Hey, don't you know that guy in the corner?" Austin looked up and saw Patrick. By the look of it, women were giving him all kinds of attention but he wasn't biting. "He's been here for about an hour." Austin said, "Joe, that's what love will do to you. Make you feel good when things are great and make you feel like shit when they're bad." He got up and walked over to Patrick. "I guess the first round is on me." Patrick slightly smiled and said, "Yeah whatever you get me, make it a double." "How you holding up son?" "Mr. Roberts, I know Thomas was your boy but that was fucked up man. I mean, I don't wish death on anyone, but

158

that was fucked up. I proposed to her Mr. Roberts. I was faithful. I just knew I was doing the right thing. I don't know what to do. I just don't understand. My body and my soul are pulling me in different directions and I'm lost. I really want to do right but I just don't know what to do. Can you help me without choosing sides Mr. Roberts?" Confused and lost himself, Austin did not know what to say. He just stared eye to eye with Patrick. Patrick sat back and sighed. "You don't have the answer do you?" Austin went to open his mouth but he was interrupted by a lady's voice. "Do you love her?" Austin turned around and it was Cynthia. "Hey Austin." She said, making Patrick comfortable to answer. "Yes, I do. But she cheated, got pregnant and hurt me." He replied. "Well, that's a tough one huh?" She asked, looking at Austin. She sat down on the chair beside Patrick and said, "How did you show her you loved her?" Patrick looked at Austin for confirmation to reply. Austin nodded as he waited for the answer. "Well I asked her to marry me?" He said. "Did she say yes? Was she excited and surprised? Even right now you would love to give her that feeling again?" "Anyone would love to give someone that feeling again. Especially when you're in love." He explained. Cynthia looked at Patrick and said, "Listen. I want you to listen clear. Have you ever broke anything when you were a kid, a teenage?" "Yeah, I broke my leg doing a back flip off some swings." He said as he chuckled. "How old were you? How was the weather outside when it happen?" "What does the weather have to do with it? He asked. "Just tell me." "It was in the winter I was about 11or 13 years old." "Ok, great." She said. "Now when you broke your leg, it hurt like hell I bet. You couldn't walk, couldn't sleep comfortably and most importantly you were a young man and summer was right around the corner. During the process of getting better, those weeks and months were bad. You had to deal with being sore and hurting more. Honestly, you probably thought that your leg wasn't ever going to get better in time for the summer. Now listen to this. You knew that summer was coming and you wanted to be out having fun. So what did you do?" Cynthia asked Patrick. "I got better." He said. "No, you didn't just get better, you worked and gained your strength back. You had to put pressure on that leg and deal with the pain. You had to work at it day after day after day. After the hard work, pain and the pressure you put on your leg, you took your first step. Then, it was another step, and another step. Once you mastered that pain and mastered walking it began to be nothing but the normal walking, running, jumping etc. Now, years later, it's like it never happened. Look, I can't tell you to go back to this woman and make it work. But if you think you can deal with this pain and work towards learning how to walk again, I'd say chance your love baby boy." Patrick looked at Cynthia and said, "I don't know you, but thank you. I guess now I have something to think about. Mr. Roberts, I'll talk to you later." Patrick said as he got up and left the table. "So, you're a philosopher now?" Austin asked Cynthia. She smiled. "No, love is pain and I have my words of glory from time to time." "Yeah, I see. Shit, you had me feeling like a student. So what are you doing here? I didn't think I'd see you this soon." "Well, I was hungry and the wings here are great. I wasn't going to speak but Joe told me I shouldn't be rude. So, hi. Now I have to go." "Wait, what's the rush?" He asked. "Umm,

160

my wings are done." She said as Joe signaled to Cynthia pointing at her bag. "You think we can just talk for a few minutes?" Austin asked. "Look Austin, I'm still confused about last night. Honestly, the only reason I came over was because Joe told me you were having a bad day." "So you think coming over here and leaving was going to make me feel better? "He asked. "No, but maybe me telling you that I enjoyed myself last night would. Well, other than the mishap. I figured that I can say, maybe we can hang out sometime down the line." Austin sipped his drink and said, "Yeah, down the line sometime." "Look Austin, I'm just trying to be nice. I'll leave you to yourself." Cynthia stood up and walked off without giving Austin a chance to say anything. She grabbed her food and looked at Austin as they made eye contact. Disappointment was written on Cynthia's face as she really didn't want to leave. But she walked out of the bar. Austin stayed at the bar for a few more hours. Then headed to the hotel where he finally passed out from drinking.

CHAPTER 10

The next morning, Cynthia was tense trying to determine whether she should go back to work. "What will I do if I lose this job? Would Austin really help pay my mortgage like he'd promise? What's the worst that could happen? I get into a fight and then fired." Running through her thoughts, she came to her senses and stopped debating. She hopped in the shower and made her way to work. She tried to convince herself that she had done the right thing. As she was leaving her car in the parking garage, she noticed Vicky's car was parked in a different space. That made the hairs on her neck stand up. Once she made it to the door her attitude switched from worried, to almost afraid, to immediately defensive. "Good morning." she said to the front desk employees as they looked shocked to see her. "Umm, good morning Ms. Heights." they replied. Cynthia got onto the elevator and headed to her office. "Ding!" The elevator door opened and it seemed like a normal day. Everyone was working and Cynthia headed to her office. Before she could get to her office, she saw Vicky eyeing her. Cynthia raised her eyebrows and rounded her eyes before walking into her office. While Cynthia was gathering her paperwork, Vicky eased her door opened and said, "Well look who's nice and early. The back stabbing bitch herself, Ms. Heights."

"There's not going to be too many bitches getting thrown my way Vicky." Cynthia said. "Yeah, maybe not, but I damn sure have plenty of reasons to throw these hands your way." Cynthia sighed with no worries. She looked at Vicky and said, "No you don't." "Well tell me bitch, give me one reason why I shouldn't come over there and drag your ass out that chair and through this office." Cynthia smiled and said, "Because you did this to yourself. Remember the guy's wallet I had, it was Austin's. He dropped it and you were the one who egged me on to make a move." "So he's been cheating with you and running around like he's a saint?" Vicky asked, relieved to have some fuel to get Austin back. "No, no, no." Cynthia said, getting up from her chair to lean on her desk. "Listen Victoria, I met your husband and Thomas before I knew you or knew you were his wife." "That's why you cried when I told you Thomas had died. You bitch! You were playing me!" Vicky said with anger. Cynthia looked at Vicky and said, "Once again, you played yourself. I had no intentions of doing anything about you running around with your 'Mr. Smith.' I could care less but me and Austin became close friend." "Did you fuck him?" Vicky asked, still lost in the situation. "No, I didn't. What is it with you and sex? I met Austin at a bar. He dropped his wallet so I contacted him. He was so in love with you. Whenever I tried to do anything sexual, he would decline and talk about you. Then Thomas died. Instead of being with him, you were getting dog fucked in a hotel by the same person that claimed to be a very close friend to him. I used to go to the bar and tell him how my boss was such a cheater, not knowing it was your husband. So when I got to your house and seen that man... That great guy... That someone that could love and respect a women like he did you... I saw that he was getting dragged through the mud by the people who were supposed to be supporting him after his best, best, best friend was just taken away from him. I knew then you guys were the kind of people that I didn't want to be around. And the crazy thing is, you never told me Andrew's real name. I only knew him as Mr. Smith. I didn't tell or say shit. You did all of this to yourself." Vicky was very angered and heart broken. Not because she was mad at Cynthia, but because Cynthia was right. "Look Vicky, I understand exactly what you're going through. This was never my intention, I swear." Vicky walked from the door of the office and said, "Women don't do things like this over a man unless they're in love." Cynthia looked at Vicky with guilt written on her face. Vicky then said, "But that's another story. And yes Cynthia, I do know you understand me and my ways." "What are you talking about Vicky?" Cynthia asked curiously. "Well, when you told me that your cousin or family member had died a few months back, I looked into it. I was going to do something nice for you. Get a painting of them or a picture of some kind. I knew you were from Miami, so I called and spoke to some family members. They told me that no one died." Cynthia's eyes got big. "Who did you speak to?" She asked. "Oh, your ex-husband. He seemed nervous, but no worries. He was very kind and didn't say anything bad nor out of the way... the first conversation." "What do you mean the first conversation, how many times have you talked to him? What did he tell you?" Cynthia asked. Vicky smiled and said. "How many times shouldn't be the question, how often do we talk is more like it." Cynthia looked at Vicky and asked. "What did he tell you?" "Well, from the look of things, we are cut from the same cloth. Hell, from what he told me, you might be more expensive material. Is it true that you cheated with married men? One got a divorce thinking you were going to marry him, only to find out you weren't? Then he ended up stabbing another man that you were cheating with who he thought was your actual husband? Oh, and don't let me forget that you tried to put a hit out on your husband to get the insurance money. Only thing was, the guy lived and it wasn't your husband. That kept you from going to jail, but exposed you to a divorce. It's crazy how people can become friends and just give away information." Cynthia looked at Vicky as if she could kill her. But she calmly sat back into her chair and said, "So, you know my past. What is that supposed to mean? What is that going to prove or solve? What is your move, Vicky?" Vicky slightly smiled. "My move? Now I don't have any more moves. This is checkmate because I do know that the only reason people break marriages is because they're in love with someone who is married. You're in love with my husband, but I know that you would never tell him what I know. How do you think he would act if he knew what I knew? I hope you weren't planning to run off and be with him." Vicky laughed and said, "Let me tell you something. I know I was wrong but you want to break up my marriage and run off with my husband? Either I get him or neither one of us gets him." Then Vicky walked out of the office, only to see Jasmine. "Baby, what are you doing here? What happened? What's wrong?" In tears Jasmine said. "It's daddy. He got shot! He's in the hospital. I called you but you didn't pick

165

up." "I'm here now, let's go." They rushed to the hospital terrified for Austin, not knowing his injuries." A worker came and knocked on Cynthia's door. "Come in." She said. "Good morning Ms. Heights. I have the paperwork for the new project. How's your day going?" "It's been a little rough." "I bet not as rough as Mrs. Roberts." "Why? Why would you say that?" The employee looked at Cynthia and asked, "You didn't hear? First someone in the office exposed her at her cookout saying that she was cheating on her husband and then not too long ago she and her daughter ran out because the poor man got shot." "What! Shot! Do you know what hospital or what happened?" Cynthia asked. "No, no one knows." "Ok, thank you." Cynthia said as the employee walked out. She immediately texted Austin, "please tell me you didn't get shot, please respond back. Please tell me you're ok Austin please." Austin didn't reply. Jasmine and Vicky walked into the hospital. Vicky walked to the nurse's station and said, "I'm looking for my husband. Austin Roberts. Do you know where he is?" "He just came in a few minutes ago. He just went into in surgery but I don't know when he's getting out." Hours passed and a doctor finally came out. He called for Mrs. Roberts. "Yes, I'm Mrs. Roberts and this is our daughter Jasmine, is everything ok? How is my husband?" Vicky asked while tearing up. "Calm down Mrs. Roberts, everything is fine. Your husband is a very strong man. He took three 45 caliber bullets. One to his leg, breaking his left lower femur bone. One to the shoulder area, breaking his right clavicle bone and one breaking off his right longer floating rib bone. We were glad that he didn't bleed out, but he is good now. He is out of surgery, you can see him

166

now but do not touch nor wake him. He needs his rest." "Ok doctor, I promise, we just need to see him." The Doctor said, "Great. He's upstairs, room 334B." They rushed upstairs. Jasmine went in first and Vicky walked in right behind her. "Mommy, that's not daddy. That's Andrew. What is going on? Where is my dad, mom?" Jasmine asked as Vicky was lost trying to figure it out. Jasmine and Vicky walked out of the hospital. Jasmine said. "I'm calling daddy." The phone rung.. "What's up Jas?" Austin picked up, hungover from the night before. "Daddy! Where are you?! Where are you?!" "Calm down Jas. What's wrong?" Austin asked. "I don't know daddy? Someone called and said you had got shot!" "What?!" Austin asked sitting up on the bed. "Where are you?" he asked Jasmine. "I'm heading to the house now." She replied. "Ok, ok. I'm sure you're with your mom. I'll just have to deal with her today. I'm on my way home now!" Austin grabbed his things and hopped in his car, rushing to get to his family. While Austin was on the way to the house, Vicky asked Jasmine. "Who called you and told you your father was in the hospital." "Some women called from the hospital and said we were my dad's emergency contacts." "What was the number?" Vicky asked. Jasmine showed her the number. "That's not the hospital's number. That's Michelle's other cell phone. She wanted us there to see Andrew." "Mom, Did she do this? Is she after us too?" Jasmine asked, tearing up. "I don't know baby, but the police will get her if she shot Andrew. Everything is going to be ok." Vicky said with a nervous tone. They pulled up to the house. "Let's just wait on daddy, mom." Jasmine said. "No, it's ok. Let's go in the house." Jasmine sighed nervously and said okay.

The two women walked in the house and sat down. When Jasmine went into the kitchen she yelled. Vicky rushed into the kitchen and there was Michelle sitting there with a .45 caliber handgun in her right hand and drinking a glass of wine with her left. She looked at Vicky and said, "Oh, is that my best friend in the whole wide world?" Knowing that's what Vicky always said to Michelle. She looked at Michelle and said, "Cute!" Michelle raise the gun pointing it at Vicky and said, "Bitch don't you sass me." Austin walked in the door. "Jasmine! Vicky! Where are you'll at?!" "Oh, in here in here!" Michelle yelled. Austin walked to the kitchen and seen Michelle pointing the gun. "Don't shoot Michelle, don't shot me" he said walking in the kitchen. "Look Michelle, don't do this" trying to calm her. "Austin, don't try and come in here like you're not hurt. Three long years they were cheating. Fucking around on us. Going on trips and small vacations." "What? Is this true? You told me it was almost a year or so. You were cheating for three years?" Still pointing the gun, Michelle said. "Don't forget the vacations Austin. Hawaii, Vegas, hell they even went to St. Thomas." Vicky did not say anything. She knew that if she lied, Michelle would pump her with just as much, if not more, bullets then she did Andrew. "Answer me!" Austin yelled. "Yes Austin, we took trips and crept around town." Austin was hurt and he began not to care if Michelle shot Vicky. But then, that would mean that Jasmine wouldn't have her mom. So he started to convince Michelle to lower the gun. "Look Michelle, I know this is bad. What they did was bad but if you do this, Jasmine won't have a mom. And look, I know what you did to Andrew. I can call some people, we can get you

off. You can walk away with a slap on the wrist."
Nervously, Michelle started to think about what Austin
was telling her. Her hand started to shake as she pointed
the gun at Vicky. "You bitch! You crushed my life, my
world and you were supposed be the one I trusted."
Michelle shouted. She lowered the gun but still had it
pointed at Vicky. Michelle said, "Trust is everything, we
trusted each other with lies and secrets." Vicky tried to
make a step towards Michelle but Michelle raised the gun
saying, "Bitch, I dare you to take another step towards
me." Vicky stepped back and Austin asked, "What
secrets? What do you mean secrets?" "Tell him best
friend." Michelle said. "I don't know what she's talking
about Austin, she's drunk." Michelle started laughing and
said, "Well hey, drunk minds speak truthful words. Now
tell him bitch before I make you handicapped. You know
what? Let me speed this up. Austin, when Vicky had
Jasmine did you get a blood test?" Jasmine looked at
Vicky and said, "Mom, tell me she's lying." Austin looked
at Vicky and grabbed her by her neck, slamming her into
the fridge. "Is Jasmine my daughter?!" "That was the
reaction I was looking for!" Michelle yelled out. Looking
at Austin, Jasmine screamed. "Stop daddy, stop!" Austin
let Vicky go and Jasmine teared up asking Vicky. "Is it
true? Is daddy not my daddy?" Tears started to fall down
Vicky's face. "No, Austin is not your father." Jasmine face
turned red as she started to cry. "Aunt Michelle, can I
please go, can I go." Michelle looked at Jasmine and said,
"Baby, this will all be over soon. Just take a seat." The
whole kitchen was mad at Vicky. Not knowing what to do,
she said. "Just kill me. I know I'm a bad person." "No, not
yet. Tell Austin when you found out." Vicky didn't say

anything. Then Michelle yelled. "Now Vicky!" "Ok I will. You shut up!" Vicky screamed at Michelle. "No, no, no. You have this all wrong. I have the gun. Now tell Austin when you found out and why you didn't tell him." "I won't bitch. You can just kill me now." Michelle laughed and said, "See Jasmine, her selfish ass rather die than tell the truth. But I know what will make her talk." Michelle then pointed the gun at Jasmine's head. "If you don't tell him bitch, you both won't have any kids." Vicky yelled out. "I don't know who your father is Jasmine." In tears, she crumbled out. "I'm sorry baby." Jasmine was hurt and Austin was just in shock. "Austin looked at Michelle and asked, "Can you please go everything is crushed here. Please just let us be. Please. I'm hurting just like you. And you held this in which makes you just as bad as Vicky." Michelle smiled and said. "I'll see you around Vicky." Then left through the back door. Jasmine walked up to Vicky, slapping her, and ran to her room like a school aged kid. Austin looked at Vicky and said, "You deserved that." Then he walked into his room and started packing his clothes. "Where are you going? We need you." Vicky cried out. "This is all your mess, your friends are pulling guns out on us and pointing them at our daughter. I mean, at your daughter. Jasmine is not even my daughter?" "I can explain." Vicky said trailing Austin through the house. "You can't explain shit!" Austin yelled. "I've never put my hand on a women, but you made me do it. I don't drink and want to cheat on someone, but you make me want to. You've crushed this family, well before you knew it. What you're not understanding is this here. It's nothing to come back from." Austin started walking backwards to the closet when he heard. "Pop, pop." They stopped. "What was that?" Vicky asked. "Fucking gunshots! Where is Jasmine?" "In her room I think." Vicky said, trailing Austin as they went to check on Jasmine. She was not in her room. Austin went to check the back, while Vicky walked to the front of the house. "Austin!" Vicky yelled! He rushed to the front of the house only to see Jasmine laying on the ground. Michelle was holding the gun and pacing back and forward in tears yelling. "I thought she was Vicky! I'm sorry Jas. I wouldn't have hurt you." Vicky was on the ground holding Jasmine. "Hold on baby, Hold on." Jasmine was gasping for air. "We need to get her to the hospital. She's not going to make it if we wait for an ambulance." Austin picked Jasmine up, taking her to his car. He told Vicky to get in the back with Jasmine. Before he pulled off, Michelle and Vicky made eye contact. Austin heard another pop and saw Michelle hit the ground. Austin looked back at Vicky. She was in shock seeing her best friend of many years kill herself. Austin pushed the gas to the floor heading to the hospital and calling 911. "911, I have my daughter in my car. We are headed to MCV. She has been shot twice in her side. I'm about fifteen minute out, her name is Jasmine Roberts." "Ok, I have contacted the hospital. They know you're on your way." They pulled up to the hospital. Patrick was paged to the emergency room for a women with gunshot wounds. He did not know who it was. Patrick looked at the nurse and said, "Fill me in. I need all information." The nurse said, "Female, two gunshot to the left side of her body. She's in critical condition. Age twenty-four, name Jasmine Roberts." "Jasmine Roberts!" Patrick repeated. "Yes." The nurse said. "That's my fiancé." The nurse handed Patrick the clip board and they both rushed to the emergency room entrance. "Please lord, let it be someone else." But he saw Austin grabbing her out of the car. Patrick ran up, helping Austin and putting her on the stretcher. "Where to go?!" Austin yelled. Patrick tried to push through to head to the ER but Austin moved him out the way. Patrick tried again but Austin was pushing him away, interfering. Patrick pulled Austin away from the stretcher onto a near wall. Looking Austin in his eyes and yelling." Look got dammit I got her." Then he lowered his voice, "I got her Mr. Roberts." He released Austin running to catch up to the stretcher making their way to the emergency room. Hours passed before Patrick came out and sat on the floor. Austin and Vicky saw him and rushed over. Patrick told them that she had flat lined twice, but she pulled through." He burst into tears and said, "I thought I'd lost her." Austin and Vicky both dropped to their knees holding Patrick saying, "Thank you, thank you." They all stood up. Patrick asked what happened. They explained how Jasmine was shot by Michelle. While they were explaining, Austin came back to his senses. "It's your fault Vicky. It's all your fault. All of this is happening because of you. You ran around fucking everyone. You're an evil bitch. Vicky, you almost cost our daughter... no, your daughter, her life." Then Austin walked off to find a seat down the hall. When he pulled his phone out, he had many texts from Cynthia. He replied. "I'm not shot. That was another person. It's been a very long day. I'm not sure what to do at this point in my life. But to let you know I'm ok." Patrick walked up to Austin and took a seat right beside him. "Long day huh, Austin?" Patrick asked. "Yeah, too long of a day. So this is what you do when you run off and tell us you have to go to the hospital. You're saving lives?" Austin asked. "Yeah, this is what you got me off the streets to do. I went from being, a nobody who sold drugs to saving lives. Mr. Roberts, I want you to know that you saved my life man. I was in the streets bad, but you had faith. Thanks." "You're welcome son." Austin said. "No, you don't get it. The plug had killed all his small time and upcoming dealers. He was a rat. That was years ago. I didn't get caught up in it because of you. I just wanted to say thank you again. There's something else I've thought about today." "What's that?" Austin asked. "I'd rather have a broken leg that can be healed then to not have a leg at all." "So what are you saying son?" "When Jasmine flat lined and we got her back, it was great. But when she went out the second time, I realized that I want to fix my broken leg and marry Jasmine." Austin looked at Patrick and said, "I'm proud of you. I would love to have you as my son." Patrick got up and walked away. "Hey Patrick?" "Yes Mr. Roberts." "Don't you ever put your hands on me like that again" He said. Patrick smiled. "Yes sir." Austin got up and walked the opposite way, checking his phone but still haven't received any text back from Cynthia. Vicky caught up to Austin. "Austin! Austin! Wait up!" She said. Finally Austin turned around. "What Vicky? Haven't you done enough?" "Yes, more than enough. Look Austin, I do love you man. I really do. I know it's going to take some time, but just believe that what I did was flat out stupid. I would never do anything like that again." Austin just looked at Vicky with a blank face. "Look Austin, I know you're mad, but with all that just happened, can I just have one last hug." Vicky looked at

Austin tearing up and inch her way slowly into his arms. They held each other as Vicky said, "I thought we lost Jas today, I really did." "Well, we didn't." Austin said, still holding Vicky. Then she looked at Austin and snuck a kiss in. Austin looked at Vicky and said, "That was the last kiss you will ever get from me." He released her and turned around when he saw Cynthia. Who had just seen him hugging and kissing Vicky. She turned around and Austin ran after her. When he got down the hall, she was gone. Vicky saw how Austin ran after Cynthia and she despised it. Vicky had plans for Cynthia, way before this random encounter at the hospital. But her mission was to get her husband back. Austin went out to look for Cynthia in the parking deck. Finally, he found Cynthia getting into her car. "Cynthia! Cynthia!" He called out. Austin ran towards the car, catching Cynthia before she closed her door. "Wait, can you just talk to me? It's not what it seems." Austin said. "Yeah, that's what I used to say." Said Cynthia. "What's that supposed to mean?" Austin asked. "Look Austin, I know how it goes. You come kick it with me and then kick it with her. You know you're going back to your wife, so why front like you're not? I know the game. I've played it." Cynthia yelled. "Hold up, get out the car." Austin said while pulling the door. "What's all this shit about you played the game. You use to say this and use to say that." Cynthia didn't say anything as she looked at Austin. "Ah naw, don't your ass get all quiet now. What does that shit mean Cynthia?" He yelled. Scared, Cynthia said, "Nothing." Austin looked Cynthia in her eyes. "You're another Vicky aren't you?" "No, no, I'm not like her I swear. I just didn't know what was what at the time." What the hell does that mean Cynthia? Stop

174

talking in codes. Tell me what's going on." Austin demanded. "Nothing, it doesn't make any sense for me to tell you my past." "I like you Cynthia. I don't know how it got this way so fast but I do." He said. "You don't like me Austin, I don't deserve you." she said. "Why? Just tell me why. I'm sure we can talk our differences out." Austin said. Tearing up, Cynthia said, "Yes." "Yes what?" Austin asked. "I don't deserve you, because the answer to your question is Yes, I am like Vicky, maybe worst." Austin looked confused. "You said your husband cheated on you. That's not on you, that's on him. Whatever he did to have you thinking you did something for him to cheat is a lie, that's on him." Austin tried to explain. "No, you're not hearing me Austin, I cheated on him. My ex-husband wanted a family, the house, the Christmas picture and the whole perfect married life. He was a great man, almost as good as you. I cheated on him more than once, with more than one man. I was wrong. I got caught because I met a guy named Elmo. I cheated with Elmo and he wanted to give me what my husband wanted me to have. I loved having someone who wanted me and cared for me like my husband did. It was like I never ran out of good men. When my husband would go out of town for business, I would have Elmo in our house, playing house with him. He loved it, but I liked it. But it all went downhill when one of the other guys I was cheating with got caught. His wife found his side chick phone and I was the only number in it. He said his wife threaten to find out who I was and tell my husband. So I had no choice but to tell all my guys that it was over. I loved my husband and didn't want to get caught because I realized what a wonderful man I had. Only one thing

175

was wrong, Elmo didn't want to stop. One day, the other man I was cheating with came over when my husband was out of town. Not to fuck or anything, but to figure out a way to get him out of the mess with his wife. It was summer time and it was a nice night out. We sat on the back deck with a bottle of wine, just thinking of how crazy and how scared we were of his wife popping up on us. It was a farewell kind of night. I'll never see you again kind of thing. We talked and we never figured out a way to help him so we traded laughs as we ended the night. After the good-byes, he left my house. Before he pulled off, I heard a loud scream. I rushed outside and the man who was standing there, wasn't the man who had just left my house. It was Elmo standing in front me with a bloody knife. He rushed over to me and I was shocked and scared for my life until he said, "Baby, I don't want you to have to worry. I'll do anything for us to work out." I stood at my front door in shock. I knew everything was over for me. I just couldn't think of anything but my husband. How sweet my husband's lips tasted at our wedding and I could hear him telling me his vows. I saw us sitting on this big soft couch, looking at a movie one night as he told his friends he was staying in to spend time with me. I saw the most amazing guy, that gave me a ring, and I choose the insane fling. All for some sex. At that point in my life, I realized that I will always be faithful to the one I'm with." Austin just stood there, looking at Cynthia as she wiped her face and got into her car. "Did he kill him?" Austin asked. "No. He stabbed him in the leg and his side. I told the cops everything, but that was years ago." Cynthia said. "Have you heard from Elmo?" "Who knows what that man is thinking about now. Especially with him getting out soon." "You lied to me Cynthia. I trusted you, and you lied to me." Austin said. Cynthia looked at Austin and said, "A lie to help me. And the truth to help you. Be glad, because sooner or later Andrew would have been watching the game on your TV and drinking your beer with your slippers on." She shut her door and pulled off as Austin stood there, looking at her car drive away.

Chapter 11.

Heartbroken, Austin sighed as Vicky walked out from the shadows. "I haven't seen you look that emotionally burnt out since Gina Caine broke your heart in 1989." She said. Austin looked at her and said, "Well, not sure if I showed it or not. But I've been burnt out ever since I found out my wife had been fucking a friend of mine." Vicky looked at Austin and asked. "Are you done?" "What did you just say to me?" Austin said stepping towards Vicky. "I said, are you done? I fucked up and I know I have to deal with it, but why is it so hard for you to forgive me? Why can't we move on?" Austin looked at Vicky and said, "Just two weeks ago I was trying to get in touch with you and I had no idea where you were. I thought to myself, you were just busy. I tried to think of anything you could be doing. I tried to come up with a good reason you weren't picking up your phone. I know you have all these new clients, so I thought maybe that was it. But you weren't with clients. You were out creeping on me. I mean, you had all the boxes checked and all the details iron out on what you were doing and where you've been. The part you're not understanding is, I believed you. Every word you told me. Now I'm done. You don't get any more chances. You want to know why, Vicky?" Vicky stood there with a blank face. "It's not because you got caught, but because you were that good. You had me looking like a fool." He started to walk off. "From the sound of it, your little friend Cynthia was just that good too." Vicky blurted out at Austin. He looked back and said, "Yeah, you're right. But she moved passed it and learned from her mistakes. Not you. If you could find another way to please your selfishness, you would do it. You lose Vicky. You lose." Austin turned around and walked towards his car. Pissed and very salty about how things were turning out, Vicky stormed away. She thought to herself, "I may have lost the battle, but I will win the war." Austin headed back into the hospital to check on Jasmine. The nurse told him that it was too soon and she still needed her rest. So he decided he would sit around for a few hours, just to make sure things went well. He finally got to see Jasmine. She was sleeping and breathing just fine. "Jas. Can you hear me? Baby, I love you. I'm sorry all this is going on with your mom and me, but I pray it will all get better. I pray things will work out for the best." "Me too." Vicky said as she walked in the room. "I pray for a lot of things Austin. I hope my prayers get answered." "I thought you left." He said. "Austin, my daughter is in the hospital. I'm not leaving. You just have to deal with seeing me." "How can you act like this?" Austin asked. "What does that mean?" Vicky asked. "How can you be so calm, so relaxed and careless of everything that's going on? Do you not realize that your daughter is here hurting and trying to get well all because of you? She doesn't need a shark of a woman, she needs comfort from her mother. Do you not understand? Have you not noticed that this is the real world or what just happened hours ago?" "What are you talking about?" She asked. "Vicky, your best friend just killed herself in our front yard." Vicky looked at Austin and said, "Good, that bitch almost killed my daughter." Austin was in shock as he stared at Vicky. He realized this person that he was talking to wasn't the Vicky he knew and once loved. "Who are you? I don't know what you've done with my wife, but you're not her." Austin walked passed Vicky, bumping her shoulder. He left the hospital and headed to the parking deck. There, he sat in his car trying to figure out somewhere to go. He was beginning to feel overwhelmed. Thoughts raced through his mind like, "I should just leave, drive to another state and leave everything behind." He had plenty of money and he could run his business from anywhere. But he couldn't figure out the perfect place to go. Frustrated, he craved a drink. But he did not want to go to his bar and have Joe ask him a lot of questions. He decided to just leave and get a room at the "Hyatt Place" a little outside of town. With all that was going on, he struggled to fall asleep. He decided to take a shower. He tried to find the right plan to solve everything but he couldn't come up with anything. He wondered how things would be if he did not find out about Andrew and Vicky. He thought about how he still would have no clue and be a fool. "Why did I blame, myself. Love is trusting. When you're doing nothing but trusting, you're giving 100% love. I gave my all and it wasn't enough. Sitting around hurting does nothing for me. As hard as it seems, I must move forward and just move on." Gathering his motivation, he made his way out of the shower, dried off, got in bed and dosed off. A few hours passed when Austin was awakened by a door slamming in the hallway. He hopped up when he saw the clock read eight thirty-two p.m. Hoping to see Jasmine before visiting hours ended, he quickly through on his clothes. Rushing down to the elevator, he ran into a man, knocking his bag over. "Oh man, I apologize." Austin said, grabbing the man's bag off the floor. The man smiled at Austin with one of the creepiest smiles and said, "Its ok, these small accidents happen all the time."

Austin smiled back, handing the man his bag and said, "You smell nice, what are you wearing?" The man said, "It's 1 million by Paco Rabanne, it's the gold bottle." "It smells nice. "I'll have to buy me some." He made his way onto the elevator telling the man, "If I see you downstairs tomorrow I'll buy you a round for the accident." "I don't drink anymore." The man said when the elevator doors closed and Austin was back on his mission to see Jasmine. He raced down to the hospital praying he'd still had time. Before he got out of his car, he saw Vicky walking from the hospital on the phone. She seemed to be in a hurry but Austin paid it no mind as he just wanted to avoid her. She got in a car and it pulled off. He hurried into the hospital, going to the nurse's desk. "Hi, I know it's late but I really need to see my daughter." "May I ask who she is," the nurse said. "Jasmine, Jasmine Roberts. Her boyfriend is Patrick. Dr. Patrick." "Oh yes." The nurse said. "We only allow one person to see her or stay overnight and it looks like your wife told the other nurse that she's gone for the night. So, yes. Mr. Roberts, I will need to see your I.D and then you would be able to go see her." Austin showed the nurse his I.D and she showed him to the room Jasmine. Austin walked in the room and watched Jasmine sleeping, laying still with the I.V's in her veins and the heart monitor peeped. He stood over her bed and looked at her as he started rubbing his hands on her head. "Daddy?" Jasmine asked softly, "Yes, yes, baby I'm here." Austin's eyes began to water up from hearing Jasmine's soft voice. "Daddy, you're tearing up like a little girl." Jasmine said, joking with Austin. He wiped he eyes and said, "No baby, I was yarning before you woke up." Jasmine smiled then said, "Ouch!" as she tried to laugh threw her pain. "No, no. Try not to move baby. You have to get well, it will take some time but you will get well. I'm sorry, I'm sorry you're in this mess. I could have talked to Michelle. I could have calmed her down. And I should have made sure she had left. I should have walked her out myself." Austin said, blaming himself for Jasmine's injuries. "Can you give me some water?" Jasmine asked. "Yes baby" he said, handing her a cup. Drinking the water to clear her throat. "Daddy, You can't blame yourself. Mom did this. She cheated, not only on you but on me as well. We would have been such a happy family if she gave you her all. It's not your fault daddy. I tried not to hate her for not telling me you're not my father. And for her not wanting to have any more kids while I was growing up, it was awful. Daddy you could of had your own family and a real daughter but you were tricked into thinking I was yours. I just don't get it. How cruel can one person be?" Austin looked at Jasmine and said, "I understand, but I will always be your real father and you are my daughter no matter how you look at it. I helped you become who you are today and that's one thing no one can tell me I didn't do. You have to forgive your mom on your own time. I love you Jas, and I will always love you. I'll be here all night, right over there in that chair. If you need anything, just let me know." He went to sit down in the chair but before he could leave Jasmine's side she said, "Dad, there's something I should tell you." "What is it baby girl?" "When mom was in here she didn't know I was up. I heard her telling me that she was going to make everything better, no matter what she had to do. Then she went on talking about how people should stay in their place and how they have to learn that their actions have a reaction. I don't think she was talking about doing anything nice. Her voice and tone was in rage." Austin looked at Jasmine. "Your mom is just mad. A lot has happened in these last few weeks and she just wants things to be back to normal. But she know it's not going to be easy to do it. Now I'll be over there in the chair, get some rest, and I'll see you in the morning." Austin went and sat in the chair until he dosed off. The nurse entered the room the next morning, waking Austin. "Oh, sorry to wake up Mr. Roberts. I'll be quick, just checking Jasmine's I.V making sure she didn't pull anything out while she was sleeping." "It's ok." Austin said yarning and stretching his arms. "Do you need another pillow?" The nurse offered. "No, no, I'm fine. Thank you." He said as he stood up looking down at his phone. He notice he had seven missed calls. "How long would it be before Jasmine comes home?" Austin asked the nurse. "It's not up to me to decide, the doctor will be the one to tell you. Umm Doctor Patrick, you know him right?" The nurse asked. "Yeah, yeah. I do, he's family." He said looking at Jasmine. "Oh, that's wonderful. He's a great doctor and he will be the one who will give you the answers to any questions you may have. I'll be outside at my station if you need anything." "Thanks again." Austin said as the nurse made her way out of the room. Austin realized that Vicky could be coming anytime soon and he didn't want to deal with her. He walked over to Jasmine's bed, grabbing the pen and the note pad. "Be back soon, went to grabbed some clean clothes and shower. Didn't want to wake you. Be strong, Dad." He placed the note in Jasmine's hand and covered it with the sheets. Making sure it was out of sight in case Vicky came in. Austin headed to the parking deck where he ran into Patrick. "How are you holding up Mr. Roberts? Patrick asked. "Well, I'm doing good. Very good because of you." "Thanks a lot, but you did this Mr. Roberts. If not I would have been running them streets and this might have never happened. I would not have been able to save someone I love, or someone that anyone loves for that matter. Patrick thought to himself for a moment as he shook his head. "Why did Michelle shoot Jasmine? She loved her like she was her own." "Yes, yes. I know Patrick. She was trying to kill Vicky for having an affair with Andrew." "What? Mrs. V and Andrew? All man, that means..." "Yes Patrick that means Vicky was messing around." "Damn Mr. Roberts." Patrick said while looking at the ground. He quickly looked up and asked, "So, what happened to Michelle? Is she locked up or is she still looking for Mrs. V?" "After she shot Jasmine by mistake, she figured that Jasmine wasn't going to make it and she..." Choked up, Austin just stared at Patrick. "What happen Mr. Roberts?" Patrick asked. "She killed herself in my front yard. We were backing out of the driveway, rushing to get Jasmine here and she shot herself." Austin explained. "What? She's died. That's horrible. She was such a nice lady." Austin's phone rang. "Austin, how are you? This is Sargent Johnson. I need you to come down to the station and answer some question about the shooting." "Yeah, I was expecting your call Johnson. Give me a second to get myself together and I'll make my way to you in about an hour or so." "Not trying to sound rude. I mean, you know I have respect for you Austin. But I need you here sooner than an hour. We need to be more on my time than yours." "Sargent Johnson demanded. "Yes, yes, I understand. I'm leaving

185

the hospital now. I'll swing by the station on my way home." "Thanks a lot. I'll see you soon." "Patrick, I have to go. You take care of my daughter and keep me updated." "I will Mr. Roberts." They both turned and went their separate ways. Austin got into his car and headed to the police station. He was questioned for about three hours and had to write a statement for the record. After the police session, he finally made his way home. It was still yellow police tape around his trees and mail box. He got out of the car and walked to the house as a cold chill ran up Austin's back. He stepped over the blood stains from Jasmine and Michelle. Trying to avoid Vicky and hoping she would not pop up on him. Austin knew he had to rush. As he got over the sight of the blood stains, he opened the door and went straight to the bedroom. He grabbed all of his suits, ties, and dress shoes, throwing them in a nearby suitcase. He headed right for the front door when Austin looked back, a vision of them all having fun together came to him. Michelle, Andrew, Vicky, Thomas and himself, were all there playing cards, waiting to grade some random chick Thomas had called over. Following that image of a happy time reality had rained down on Austin, causing him to take a deep breath, shutting the door on his past. Deep down, he was filled with pain from a tug of war of heartbreaks. Struggling to get his thoughts together, he finally dragged his bags to his car and drove to the hotel. Still emotional about the scene from his house, he walked slowly to the hotel entrance. The doors opened and it was the man from before. "Hello again." Austin spoke with a soft tone. "Hi, glad I wasn't rushing, it could have been another luggage incident." The man said. "Huh? Oh yeah." Austin said

186

finally getting the joke. "I'm Austin." Austin said as he stuck his hand out." "Austin, I'm Stacy, Stacy Jones." The men shock hand as Stacy said, "You're not looking too good Austin." "Yeah, I just need some sleep. It's a lot going on man." As the elevator door opened again, Austin said. "I'll see you around Stacy." "Yeah, see yah." Stacy said as the elevator door shut. He quickly got to his room, opened the door and sat on the bed. He noticed a sign hanging on a fridge that mentioned the room's mini bar. Curious, Austin opened the fridge where he discovered several miniature liquor bottles. Excited, Austin grabbed a bottle of scotch and gulped in down in one sip. He took his clothes off to take a quick shower so he could hurry back to indulge in the mini bar. Austin finally found a sense of relaxation, as the alcohol numbed his body and he fell into a deep sleep. He had a dream about Thomas. Thomas was walking and talking to him on an open road but he could not hear him. He tried his best to get Thomas's attention but Thomas wouldn't stop walking and talking. Then Thomas stopped and said, "People are not the same, they can change." A car started driving towards them. Vicky was in the driver's seat honking the horn while running over Thomas and Austin. Austin jumped up. He was covered in sweat and dehydrated from the liquor. Freaked out about the dream, Austin got some water and turned on the T.V. He watched it until he dose off again, and he slept until morning. After that crazy dream, he decided that he would try avoid Vicky. He did so for about a week. Then one Monday morning, Vicky showed up at Austin's job with breakfast. "Good morning handsome." She said. "What are you doing here? Did Kyle let you in? You trying to get that kid fired aren't you?" Austin yelled. "No Austin, no. I come in peace." Vicky said, walking over to Austin's desk and sitting in a chair. "Look, just hear me out. Have breakfast with me and by the time we're finished, I'll be ready to leave." "What if I don't have the time? What if I just flat out say no?" He asked. "Then I will go back to being a bitch. You know how I can act up in here." Austin sat back in his chair and stared at Vicky. Then he grabbed the sandwich because he did not want the drama. "You have until the end of the sandwich to get everything out." Vicky smiled. "I'm glad you decided to play along. I didn't want to have to act like a bitch. It's too early for all of that. Austin, I know I did you wrong. I know I hurt you deeply. I just wanted tell you I'm sorry and that I hope we could work things out. Of course not right away, but I do hope we can. I also want you to know that I understand if you don't want to make things work." Choking on her words, she said, "I won't fight you. I'll sign the divorce papers if we ever take it that far. I just want you to know that I am really sorry and I apologize for all the pain I've caused you. I mean that from my heart. You know, I was just being dumb and greedy. Not realizing what I had in front of me." Austin was in shock. He was not expecting Vicky to say that. He was not expecting her to be so apologetic. He cleared his throat and said, "Thank you. I think with everything that's going on. That was the nicest thing you've said to me. I must be honest though. I don't think right now I'm in a position to state what I want. I do thank you for coming and really being a women about this, but I'm still pissed at you. I'm still emotionally turned upside down and I don't know what I want to do. I mean shit, was you thinking you would just come in here and make me forgive you? Did you think that things were going to go down that easily? I thought I had a daughter. I don't Vicky. We were so happy, I was so happy. I would have been even happier if I knew your daughter was ours. It is going to be hard for me to come back to you. Too much has happened." Avoiding most of what Austin said, Vicky asked, "Is it anyone that's blocking us from being together?" Austin froze up. Vicky knew Cynthia was still a possibility. "No, it's no one." Austin said, lying through his teeth. Vicky picked up on it. "Well, Mr. Roberts, I don't want to be late for work. I have a meeting to attend. I'll just be on my way. Please enjoy the rest of your day and do think about what I've said." Vicky got up and walked out. Austin was confused. He wanted to forgive Vicky but how could he. He had been betrayed and in his mind, he has possibly found someone better then Vicky. He wasn't sure what to do so he went back to work, putting the stress behind him. Vicky walked into her building. "Good morning." She spoke proudly to her co-workers as they passed and spoke back. Continuing to strut through the building, she came to the elevator where she saw Cynthia. "Well, good morning beautiful. I hope all is well." Vicky said while smiling. Cynthia looked at Vicky. "Good morning." As she tried to figure what had Vicky so joyful. "Ding!" The elevator door opened. "After you." Vicky said. "Oh no, you're the boss." Cynthia said, waving her hand guiding Vicky onto the elevator. Vicky walked in and Cynthia followed. The two ladies stood beside each other in silence until Vicky spoke up. "Cynthia, I just wanted to say you were right. I was wrong about everything. I was wrong about cheating and creeping around. I mean girl, if I would have just listened to your warnings, none of this would have happened." Vicky tried not to tear up. "I just wish things were different and I wish I could change things." Cynthia stood there looking at Vicky, trying to read through the bullshit. Then she asked, "Why are you telling me this?" Vicky said, "Because you were right and I was so mean to you about it all. You warned me that something bad could happen. I mean, especially with what happened to you." "Oh, so this is what it's all about? You are comparing your wrongs and my wrongs. Vicky, listen. I'm nothing like you." Cynthia said. "Ding!" The elevator door opened and Cynthia stormed out as Vicky trailed her. "Cynthia!" Vicky called out. Cynthia stopped and turned around. Vicky smiled and said, "Cynthia, you're just like me." She walked closer and said, "But see, your past can teach me how to change and help me learn from my mistakes." When Vicky said that, Cynthia got a very bad vibe. She turned and walked to her office. "See you at the meeting." Vicky said as she smiled at Cynthia. Cynthia tried to figure out why Vicky was acting the way that she was. She thought maybe Austin and Vicky got back together. Or could it be that she is really trying to start over. As she thought about Vicky starting over and being honest, she chuckled to herself. She knew Vicky wasn't that honest of a women and that she had to be up to something. In order to see what was going on, she decided to text Austin. "How's Jas?" She texted. Austin replied, "She's getting well, getting stronger by the minute. I'm surprised to hear from you." Cynthia replied, "She was on my mind, so I thought I would see how she was holding up." "Is that all you wanted?" He asked. "No, has Vicky been acting funny towards you?" "Funny how?" He texted back, curious. "Austin, she's been acting nice. Telling me I was right and she was wrong. It's not like her to be nice to people that made her mad. It's kind of scary." "She did come to my job this morning and brought me breakfast. Saying she was sorry about everything. I think she just realize that life is not going her way and this is her way trying to win over karma." Cynthia knew that Austin was right about one thing, but not everything. She knew Vicky may have realized her life isn't going the way she planned. But Cynthia knew that Vicky was the type of person that will make things go as she planned. Austin texted, "Can we talk in person?" Cynthia responded with excuses. Austin asked, "Maybe tomorrow?" "I'm busy tomorrow." "Let's just have coffee in the morning and I'll leave you alone. I'll let you work your life away." Austin replied. Recognizing that Austin wasn't going to give up, she accepted. Austin was excited. Moments later, Cynthia's office phone rung. "This is Ms. Height." "Cynthia, this Vicky. I need you to meet me downstairs in the conference room." "The meeting isn't until another hour. Why do you want me to go so early?" Cynthia asked. "Like I said Cynthia, I need you to meet me downstairs in the conference room." With an attitude, Cynthia responded. "Yes boss, I'll be there in five minutes." Vicky hung up the phone without saying anything. Five minutes had passed when Cynthia opened the door and walked into the conference room. There was Vicky, sitting on the table next to a chocolate covered cake with red roses on it. The cake read, "Congratulation Cynthia Heights" in red icing. Cynthia walked closer and asked, "What is this? A joke. Chocolate icing with a small hint of poison?" Vicky stood up. "No baby girl. If I was trying to kill you. I wouldn't do it with poison." Cynthia said, "Kill? I wish you would think about killing me. Better yet, I wish you would do anything to me." "Calm down, calm down. No one is trying to hurt you. This cake does not have any kind of poison in it, but it is for you. Look, I know that we have our beef. And you did brake my marriage up. But I also know that I wouldn't have finished this deal with Witten Exports without you. They are giving you and I a bonus in the next hour and I want to personally say, thank you. I know things are going to be hard between us. I'm just trying to keep the peace and keep my job. The CEO, Mr. Stewards and his staff are coming." "Wait! Why are they coming down?" Cynthia asked. "Are you not hearing me? The deal with Witten Exports is done! We did it!" Vicky said excited. "Are you fucking with me Vicky?" Smiling Vicky said, "Bitch, I don't like you but I did buy you a cake. I'm serious!" "Oh my god! I can't believe this. Do you know what this means?" Cynthia asked. "Yes bitch, we are in the money!" "The real meeting got switched. It's on the twenty-second floor now. Let's go to the conference room were these rich men are going to give you their money". Excited, Cynthia walked towards the conference door to set up for the meeting. She would not forget for one second that Vicky admitted that there would be problems between them. But that is something that she already knew. Before exiting the room, Cynthia turned and said, "We would have been great friends." Making it known that they were not. "Well, how about you keep wishing. You do that a lot. Maybe you should wish for something and make it come true." Vicky said. Cynthia smiled, "I'm not sure if wishing to some magic genie is going to get Austin back. You need God." Then she walked out. Vicky stormed to the door and called out to Cynthia. Cynthia turned around. Then Vicky said, "Maybe I'm not wishing for him. Maybe I'm wishing for things to be as if this all never happened. I would say a prayer, but I would definitely go to hell if I prayed for what I'm wishing. Then again, wishing and praying is all the same in my eyes. But I guess when you're pulling the strings and directing, it's neither. It's more like, orchestrating." Cynthia smiled "Well good thing I'm not in your band." She turned and walked away. Folding her arms and leaning on the door, Vicky mumbled under her breath, "Like hell you're not." It was minutes before the meeting. The two women were sitting in the conference room, not saying a word to one another but held an eye staring contest. Moments later, the CEO and his staff walked in. "Ladies, ladies, Good Morning." "Good morning Mr. Stewards." They both greeted him, shaking his hand. "I wanted you two to meet someone that could bring us new business overseas. This is Emanuel Curtis." Emanuel was a six feet four inches tall, well-built handsome man. He was thirty-five years old and currently searching for a new mom for his daughter. He had his eye on Cynthia and Vicky took notice. "Good morning ladies." Emanuel stuck his hand out to Cynthia and said, "Cynthia right?" Blushing, Cynthia asked. "Yes, how did you know?" "I didn't. I was hoping you weren't Vicky, who's the married one." Mr. Stewards cut in, "Business first please." He guided Emanuel to Vicky. "Yes Mr. Stewards. You're right. So this must mean you are Victoria. Who likes to be called Vicky depending on how long you've known her." Emanuel explained. "Well yes. You are absolutely right. But we are going to make money together, so you can call me Vicky even though I just met you." They all laughed as Cynthia just smiled and nodded. "Ladies, please be seated. This will not take long." Mr. Stewards suggested. "You two women are the balls off this company. I do like the worker, but I love the enforcer. The deal you made with Witten Exports will make us millions! They have already paid a small percentage." As Mr. Stewards was talking he reached into his pocket and pulled out two white envelopes. He placed them on the table. "Vicky, you have been an asset for many years. Now you are molding a women that's just like you." Vicky quickly added, "I tell her that all the time." while looking at Cynthia and smiling. Mr. Steward continued to talk. "These are for you ladies." He slid the envelopes over. The ladies open them to see a signed check for fifty thousand dollars. In shock, because she never had anything more than three thousand dollars in her bank account, Cynthia blurted out, "Holly fuck!" Catching the attention of Emanuel. Emanuel said. "That was my first reaction to my first bonus. I thought you knew about this kind of money." He smiled. Embarrassed, Cynthia said, "Sorry, I don't. I haven't seen this in check form my entire life." Mr. Steward stood up and said, "Well, if you keep up the good work you will get used to it." Emanuel stood up and said, "Hopefully, that means you will stick around." He stuck his hand out to Vicky as Cynthia stood to join the men. "It was nice meeting you." He said shaking Vicky's hand. "And it was very nice meeting you." Emanuel said as he shook Cynthia's hand. The two men walked out. Right when the door shut, Vicky said, "Well, I'm glad you found him so you can leave mine alone." "I don't know what you talking about." Cynthia said as she walked towards the door. "Oh, you know." Vicky said. "No I don't. But you know what I do know Vicky?" Cynthia asked. "Well, since you're not in the guessing mood, I'll just tell you. I know Austin has the cutest birth mark on his inner thigh." Vicky looked at Cynthia and just smiled. "Well played." Cynthia knows she did not have sex with Austin, but she did remember seeing it when Austin was in her bathroom. "Take the rest of the day off. Go enjoy your money." Vicky said. "Thanks boss, I will." Cynthia replied and headed to the elevator. The door open and Emanuel was there waiting. "Back so soon." Cynthia said. "For a good reason." He replied. "Money is always a good reason." Cynthia stated. Emanuel smiled. "You're a good reason too. Can I take you to lunch?" He asked. Shocked and nervous Cynthia asked, "Like right now?" "Well, yes like right now. Unless Dinner is better?" He asked. Not knowing what to say, Cynthia just blurted out. "Yes, that's better." "Ding!" The elevator sounded as Cynthia rushed off. "Great, I'll get your number from your secretary." Emanuel said. "Ok." She said as she sighed nervously, turning to walk off as the doors on the elevator closed. Once inside her office, Cynthia sat in her chair and looked at her check again. "I can't believe it." She thought to herself. "Fifty-K! Thank you lord." Not knowing how to act, she gathered her things and made her way out of the office. She went straight to the nearest bank. After all she has been through, she knew it was best to save it in case she had to up and move. The evening came faster than expected as she laid in bed, resting and watching movies. Her phone went off as an unknown number popped up. "Hi. Hello?" She asked. "Hi, umm Cynthia?" The man asked on the other end. "Yes this is she." "Great! This is

Emanuel. I was wondering if eight is an ok time for us to meet." Sitting up in her bed and cleaning her throat she said. "Hi. Umm what time is it?" "Its 6:30 right now. I was trying to give you some kind of heads up. I finished up at the office a little later than I expected. Sooo, is eight okay,?" "Umm, sure." She said nervously." "Is everything ok?" He asked. "Yes, everything is fine. Where would you like to meet? She asked. "Well, this is still a legit date. But I was thinking Buffalo Wild Wings. I really don't get a chance to watch sports and I figured it would be a relaxed setting. I'm not as up tight as I seem." He explained. They both chuckled. "I hope not. And now that you mentioned it, I definitely can go for wings, a beer maybe, even a shot or two." Cynthia said. "Aww man. A women who like wings and beer. This is going to be great! Well, I know you know where the one is downtown. I'll see you there at eight." "Eight it is." "Great! I'll see you then." The next hours flew by as she hopped out the bed and showered. As she got dressed she realized she was being pressed for time. Her phone sounded as she rushed to grab it, hoping Emanuel was not already there. Unexpectedly, it was Austin. "Hey. How's your day?" Excited, she wanted to spill the news about her first bonus. She figured that it would lead to Austin asking if she wanted to celebrate with a drink or dinner, so she down played her day. " It's ok, im kind of busy." "Wish you weren't busy. It would be great to grab a drink, I miss our conversations." He responded. Cynthia found herself feeling guilty. In a way, she felt as if she was betraying Austin. She did not understand why she was feeling this way. She told Austin that she was busy and continued to head out to meet Emanuel. Cynthia found herself still thinking about

Austin. She was praying that he would not somehow pop up at the bar. Half way there, Cynthia's phone rang. It was Emanuel. "Hello?" Cynthia answered. "Hey, just checking on you, making sure you are not standing me up." Cynthia laughed. "No, no. That's bad etiquette. If I wasn't going to show up, I wouldn't have agreed to meet you. That's not me. But more good news, I'm in route. I should be there in ten minutes." "Ok, ok. That is good news. I'm already here. When you walk in come to your left. I'll be in the booth near this weird looking guy in a blue shirt." Cynthia laughed. "Why are you near some weird looking guy?" Laughing he said, "He just came over and sat right near the booth. It was extremely weird." Emanuel explained while laughing. "Well, ok." "Ok, great. See you in a short." "They hung up their phones and minutes later Cynthia arrived. While she was touching up her hair, she saw a car that reminded her of Austin's. Then another feeling of guilt came over her. She did not really want to think of Austin, but she could not get over how he would feel if he was to see her with another man. Coming around to her senses, she reminded herself that she was single. She opened her car door and headed into the bar. She walked in the bar, looking for a weird man in a blue shirt to her left. There was a man in a blue shirt, but he was definitely not weird looking. The man in the blue shirt was Emanuel. He saw Cynthia and stood up smiling. Cynthia saw Emanuel and was very amazed. She checked out his broad shoulders and fit body. She walked over. "Well, well, well. Somebody looks good without a suit." "Why thank you beautiful, I clean up well from time to time. And you, you look amazing Cynthia. Please have a seat." They both sat down. Everything was going perfect until Cynthia caught a glimpse of a man that looked like Austin. She was not sure if it was him or not, but she was extremely nervous about it. The man was sitting on a stool at the bar. When he turned around, she realized it was not Austin. She was relieved as her anxiety calmed down, but still struggled to give Emanuel her undivided attention. As Emanuel talked, she spaced away looking around the bar. She cut him off from whatever he was talking about and asked, "Have you ever found yourself liking someone that you shouldn't like?" Emanuel smiled. "No, most of the time I find myself loving someone that I shouldn't love." "That's what I meant." Cynthia said as she caught herself admitting to loving Austin. "I just don't understand. I'm single and I'm here with you, nervous that this friend of mine might walk in. I know a lot of women would love to have a man like you pay them some attention, but I don't think I can. I don't think it's you. I just think that my feelings are with someone and I can't explain why." She stood up, reached in her pocketbook and laid a fifty dollar bill on the table. "I'm sorry Emanuel. I have to go." "Cynthia!" He called out. She looked at Emanuel and said, "I'm sorry." Emanuel said, "For what? Listen, if I'm the reason you found out that you're in love. I'm thankful for that. Hopefully that will rub off on me." He grabbed her hand and placed the fifty dollar bill in it. "No women will pay for me to eat and have a good time, especially one I consider a good friend." Cynthia hugged Emanuel and said, "Thanks for understanding." "I hope I can find a women like you to be a great mom to my daughter one day." "I'm sure you will with your fine ass." She joked. Emanuel smiled. "Not fine enough huh?" The both laughed "If I didn't fall before you, I definitely would have fallen for you. You're not going to have a problem finding a woman." Looking at Cynthia, Emanuel said, "Well back to the search." "No need to search, she will come to you." Then she turned around and walked to her car. Arriving home, she took another shower and hopped back in her bed. Before falling asleep, she texted Austin. "Breakfast will be fine. How's ten a.m?" Happy to hear from her, Austin quickly replied, "Perfect, see you at ten!"

CHAPTER 12.

Yawning and stretching, Austin rolled over to turn off his screaming alarm clock. He grabbed his phone and seen that Vicky texted him, "Good morning. Did you enjoy your evening last night? He replied. "No, but I'm sure to enjoy my morning." Frustrated about Vicky but excited about Cynthia. He hopped out of the hotel bed, making his way to the shower. Austin got out, dried off and his phone sounded again. Hoping it was Cynthia, he walked over in a hurry. It was only one of his worker. Austin threw his phone on the bed and continued to get dress. He grabbed his finest suit, sharpest shirt and cleanest shoes out of the closet. Looking at the time that read eight fifty-seven a.m he thought, "I have plenty of time." So he got his things in order and headed out of his room to start his day. This day was different for Austin. He was extremely happy as he greeted those who passed by. While getting in his car, he sent Cynthia a text letting her know he was on his way. His phone fell under his car seat but he figured he would get it when he stopped for breakfast. The only thing on his mind was trying to come up with the right things to say to Cynthia. He figured he would prepare himself in case Cynthia was upfront in telling him that she did not want to have anything to do with him. He was getting close to Cynthia's house so he told himself, "Alright Austin, get it together." He pulled up to Cynthia's house, making his way to the door. Austin noticed that the door was cracked open but he did not want to be rude and just walk in. He rang the doorbell. After about ten seconds he rang the doorbell again. He figured she was in the shower and he was just going to be patient. A few more seconds passed and he grow concerned as he walked through the screen door and push the house door open. "Cynthia!" He called out, but he got no response. As he peeked his head around the door he was mortified. "Cynthia!" He yelled, as he discovered her bruised body. Her face and jaw were swollen. Her eyes were black and her body laid on the stairs, looking lifeless. Austin grabbed her, pulling her up right as he checked to see if she was alive. "Cynthia! Cynthia! Can you hear me?" He yelled. He tried to open her eyes but they just rolled in the back of her head. "Come on. Come on. Stay with me Cynthia." Austin put his ear to her mouth and nose to hear if she was still breathing. Glad and relieved, she was. Austin picked her up and ran her to the car, speeding off to the hospital. Feeling that this was becoming a routine, he pulled up screaming for help. After going through the emergency process, the doctor checked Cynthia in with minor injuries. She had fractured ribs and a bruised jaw. When she was brought into her room, Cynthia woke up from coughing. Austin heard her and walked over to the bed. "Please stop! Please stop!" She struggled to scream as she was in pain from her bruised jaw. "Calm down, calm down. Everything is ok. It's me, Austin." Relieved, Cynthia burst into tears. "Austin, I have to go, I have to get out of here." She said crying. "What? Why? What's wrong? What's going on? Do you know who did this?" Struggling to wipe her tears and sit up on the bed, she nodded her head. "Who? Tell me. I'll tell the cops." Austin said. Cynthia rolled her eyes and said, "The cops can't help me. This man found out where I was." She said. "How? And what man?" Austin asked with concern on his face. "The man I was telling you about. The man that broke my marriage up and almost had me put in jail." "Elmo?" Austin asked. Cynthia looked at Austin with fear in her eyes. "Yes, him." "Well, you can come with me." Austin said. A tear ran down Cynthia's face as she looked at Austin. Feelings of hope come upon her. She felt protected. Austin asked, "When you left Florida, who did you tell that you were moving here?" "No one. I told no one. I mean my sister knows what state, but not the city. That was her choice for good reasons." Austin began pacing back and forth trying to figure all this out. "So, you didn't tell anyone nor talk to anyone?" He asked once more. "That's it." Cynthia said as her eyes opened wide. "Vicky!" "What?" Austin asked. "Vicky, she said she called my ex-husband, but I know he wouldn't talk about me and tell all of my business. Vicky must have found out Elmo's release date and had him come here. I mean it makes perfect sense Austin." "How? What makes perfect sense? Vicky wouldn't try and kill you?" Austin said. Sitting up and pouting as tears begin to fill her eyes she said, "Austin. Elmo came to my house in the middle of the night. Grabbing me by my throat and pulling me out of my bed. I fought back the best I could, but he was so strong. It was terrifying having someone over power you. He kept saying. 'Lovely bird, I've missed you, I've missed you.' He tried to kiss me but I moved my face and that's when he smacked me to the ground. He picked me up by my hair and neck and said, 'A kiss would have been nice but I'm not here for that.' I asked him, 'what are you here for. What do you want?' He said, 'Because of you, I'm a convicted felon.' I told him that he could have a second chance at life. He asked, 'a second chance with me?' I said, 'no, just at life.' He smiled and said that life is paying me to be here and do this. Then he threw me down the stairs." Austin cut Cynthia off and asked, "How is this involving Vicky?" Cynthia said, "Because she was the only person that was contacting people from my past Austin. You have to believe me." "Ok, ok." He said still confused. "She set this up. Look at me Austin." Cynthia said. "After this man threw me down a flight of stair he pulled out a gun and he beat me. He beat me with a gun!" She yelled bursting out in tears. "And this why I know your wife has everything to do with it. After the beating, I saw him cock the gun and raised it to my face. I heard him take a deep breath and with my one opened eye, we made eye contact. He finally looked at me as if he saw me for the person I'm am. The great person I was to him. Not just the girl that was running scared from him. He lowered the gun and whispered, 'I'm sorry.' He was confused and I just laid there before blacking out. I heard him under his breath say. 'She can't pay me enough to do this.'" Austin was in shock. He was trying to figure out what to believe. He knew that Vicky could be an evil bitch, but he didn't think she would have someone try and kill Cynthia. While he was thinking. Cynthia said, "Austin. Think about it for one second. How would he know where I lived? How would he know any of this? The state I'm in. The city I'm in. Just be smart about this." She begged. Austin knew she was making sense but he needed to find out the truth. "Ok, let me go get some air, you're safe in here. I'll let the nurses know that no one is to come in or out of this room." Cynthia laid back in the bed in fear, scared to be alone. Austin walked out of the room and told the nurses what was going on, before he went to his car. He

204

grabbed his phone from under the seat and seen that he had missed a few text messages. Some were from work. The other was from Patrick with good news about Jasmine being released. Patrick planned to take her to his house until she was better. Austin was fine with that. He then texted Vicky, "Where are you?" Vicky replied. "On site for a job." Then she quickly replied "Have you heard the good news? Jasmine is coming home today." Austin was still trying to figure Vicky out. He texted back, "Yeah, great news." He was still debating if Vicky was trying to kill Cynthia or not. He started his car and informed his employee that he would have to do the project alone because Jasmine was coming home. Being the boss, they had no choice but to understand. He made his way to the hotel to get the blue prints for his job. Arriving at the hotel, Austin rushed to the elevator. "Ding!" When he got off of the elevator, he saw Mr. Jones, letting a woman that favored Vicky in his room. Not paying it much attention, Austin continued to his room to grab those blueprints. Searching high and low, he could not find them anywhere. Austin sat on the bed and took a breather. He remembered where they were. "The window sill." He thought to himself. Austin dashed to the window, relieved that they were rolled up neatly and in order. While at the window, Austin saw an all black Audi that looked like Vicky's. Then it hit him. The women did not just look like Vicky, she was Vicky. Austin threw his suit jacket off and opened the door. He made his way down to Mr. Jones' room. He put his ear to the door to see if he could hear anything. The T.V was too loud so he could not hear much. He found himself feeling paranoid. He started to second guess himself so he slowly started to head back to his room. Then he heard a women scream, but he was not sure what she said. The woman screamed again, but this time he heard her. "You fucked up! You stupid shit!" The women yelled. The door then opened and Austin jumped back so he would not be seen. Fortunately, the man grabbed the women before she walked out. The door slammed on the door stopper. They stopped yelling but continued to argue as Austin walked closer. He caught on to the voice. Sure enough it was Vicky. Vicky told the man, "You dumb shit, I'm not paying you a penny. We had a deal and that was for you to kill that bitch! I flew you up here, not to rekindle your love or be a sick stalker, but to take care of business." "Don't call me a fucking stalker! I'm not a stalker. She loved me at one point. Look lady. I did what you paid me for. You said fuck that bitch up and get rid of her. I did it. She knows I'm here so she's going to run. She always has." Elmo explained. Vicky said, "If I wanted that bitch to run, I would have convinced her to join a track team you stupid motherfucker." "Look, all I want is some of it, I don't even need the whole payment." Vicky started laughing, "You're not getting shit, not half, not whole, not even a plane ticket. You have done enough for a bus ticket." Elmo raised his voice and said, "Look bitch, I went out of my way to do this for you. Do you not remember what I did to Cynthia? And that was someone I love. I don't love you." Vicky asked, "So, what's that supposed to mean?" Elmo looked at Vicky and said, "I'm not dumb. You were going to have me kill Cynthia and put it all on me, the sick stalker." Elmo pulled out his gun and said, "No bitch. I won't get caught up in this shit. Not today. Now give me my damn money!" Vicky said, "No." Elmo cocked the gun back, but before he could make another move Austin bust in the room. He landed on the man, pushing him down as he fired a shot that went out of the window. Vicky flew to the floor as Austin grabbed the man's hand and punched him in the face. Austin managed to knock the gun out of his hand. The man fell, but Austin was pulled down with him. "Stop!" Vicky yelled out. She pointing the gun at Elmo from across the room. Elmo rolled off of Austin but not before Austin delivered one last blow, knocking Elmo out cold. Lowering the gun, Vicky asked, "What are you doing here?" "This is where I've been staying, what's wrong with you?" Austin asked. Vicky looked at Austin. "Why do you keep asking me that? You know I just want you back." He looked at Vicky. "No, you can't. That can't happen. That's not going to happen. I heard everything, you belong in jail. This man almost murdered Cynthia. Do you know that?" "Yes, Austin I do. I was the one who set it up." "She ruined us, she told everything. You don't see how happy we would have been or still would be." Austin looked at Vicky and said, "No. No I don't see how happy we would have been. The truth is, you would have kept cheating and lying about everything. You were happy. You were getting your cake and eating it too. I would have been a man that suspects something, just wouldn't be able to prove it. When Cynthia told me you were cheating. You could have just accepted the fact that you got caught like a woman and moved on. But now you're going to jail." "Well, she told on me?" Vicky said. "So I guess I can tell on her. Your little Cynthia was on a date last night. Did she tell you that?" "What?" Austin asked. "You're lying Vicky." Vicky laughed and said, "No, you want me to be. Your little Cynthia went and got her some drinks and dick last night. Things aren't as they seem Austin." "I don't believe you. You're lying and saying anything to get your way and stay out of jail. I'm telling everything. You are a reckless person and you belong in prison." Austin tried to walk out, but Vicky lifted the gun and pointed it at Austin. He stopped in his tracks. "A man cheats on his wife with a woman who has a stalker. The wife finds out and she follows her husband to the hotel where she think he's cheating. But the only thing is, the cheating girl is not in the room, the stalker is. The wife shoots the husband for cheating. She then shoots the stalker in self-defense for him trying to attack her. See, I can say I just blacked out and be free. Everyone thought I was the cheater, but No! It was Austin all along." She explained. "You are sick Vicky. Look at you. Look what you've done. All this comes from you. You cheated and made the domino effect in your life. You were a good wife, but you slept with you best friend's husband and caused her to kill herself. Your best friend Vicky! Now you have a gun pointed at the one person who loved and cared for you for twenty plus years." Vicky's eyes started to water as Austin inched his way to her. "Vicky, you have to stop." He said to her as tears finally streamed down her face. "Vicky baby. Give me the gun." He said, slowly grabbing the gun out of her hand. He turned and started to walk back towards the door. Vicky stood and cried with pain from all what she had done. "Austin!" She yelled out. Austin stopped and looked at Vicky. Vicky said, "Anyone but her, just not the women who broke my marriage up." Austin said, "Vicky, she didn't break your marriage up, you did." Austin rushed down the stairs knowing the cops were going to be on their way. He had no time to waste. He finally made it to the first floor. He snuck out of a side door to get to his car. He pulled off, racing back to the hospital. When he arrived, he went straight to Cynthia's room. Cynthia sat up in her bed as Austin walked in calmly. "What? What's wrong?" Cynthia asked. "Elmo was the guy who came to your house, but you won't have a problem with him anymore. He's gone for good." "What? You killed him?" She asked. "No, no I didn't. But I do know for a fact why he did it. I heard him and Vicky arguing over the money she was supposed to pay him to kill you." "That bitch tried to kill me? I can't believe it." Cynthia said, sitting back in her bed. "So, what about her? Is Vicky going to jail?" She asked. "Yes, I'm going to tell the cops everything. They both will go to prison. Okay. See you around." Austin said, making his way out of the room. "Wait! Where you going?" "I'm going home. I'm sure you have someone to take care of you. Besides, Jasmine came home today." "What's wrong with you? Why are you in your feelings? I'm the one that just got beat up and now laying in a hospital bed." Austin said, "Yeah, but whose bed were you in last night? Cynthia, I'm tired. The last few weeks and months have been fucking crazy and I don't need to be falling in love with another Vicky." "What are you talking about? Why are you talking to me like this?" Cynthia asked. "Look, I know you're hurt. I also know what happened last night. Before you were attacked, I know you were with someone." Cynthia sat back in the bed. "Why did you lie? Why did you have to go and fuck some dude?" Cynthia looked at Austin. "I lied because I wasn't sure. I lied because I needed to make sure I was ready, and I found out I was. Yes, I went on a date last night, but I left in the middle of it. I went home and texted you. I didn't fuck him. I didn't even kiss him. All because I found out I was in love you." She said as she laid back in the bed. "What did you say to me?" Austin asked. "I said I love you. I love you Austin and I've been fighting it. I'm sorry it took me so long to tell you." Austin just looked at Cynthia and rushed over to kiss her. "Ouch!" She yelled out. "Oh, I'm sorry." Austin said as they both laughed. The next day Cynthia was released on bed rest and as the weeks passed she got better and went back to work. The CEO Mr. Stewards, gave her the head position. As weeks turned to months, Patrick had forgiven Jasmine and proposed once more. This time, Austin got the chance to walk Jasmine down the aisle. Years passed and Austin still ran his businesses. He took more vacations to spend more time with his new wife, Cynthia Roberts. Everything started to come together until one day, Austin and Cynthia were eating dinner and the phone rang. "I'll get it baby." Austin said. "Hello?" "Well hello there? I'm guessing you know the sound of my voice." Vicky said. Austin was in shock. "How did you get this number Vicky?" Cynthia heard Austin and she rushed over to the phone. "If I can get your phone number, I can get your address. I told you, anyone but her. But no, you had to cross me." "Fuck you." Austin said, as Cynthia grabbed the phone from him. "What do you want bitch?" Cynthia asked. "I thought I took care of you along time of ago. Just know that being in here has made me realize something. If you want something done right, you have to do it yourself. So if you hear of a prison break, anywhere I'm at, just know I'm coming for you." Vicky said. "I'll be waiting bitch." Cynthia responded and hung up the phone.